THE IMPORTANCE OF BEING EARNEST
and Other Plays

Oscar Wilde

With an Introduction by
Sylvan Barnet
and a New Afterword by
Elise Bruhl and
Michael Gamer

SIGNET CLASSICS

SIGNET CLASSICS
Published by New American Library, a division of
Penguin Group (USA) Inc., 375 Hudson Street,
New York, New York 10014, USA
Penguin Group (Canada), 90 Eglinton Avenue East, Suite 700, Toronto,
Ontario M4P 2Y3, Canada (a division of Pearson Penguin Canada Inc.)
Penguin Books Ltd., 80 Strand, London WC2R 0RL, England
Penguin Ireland, 25 St. Stephen's Green, Dublin 2,
Ireland (a division of Penguin Books Ltd.)
Penguin Group (Australia), 250 Camberwell Road, Camberwell, Victoria 3124,
Australia (a division of Pearson Australia Group Pty. Ltd.)
Penguin Books India Pvt. Ltd., 11 Community Centre, Panchsheel Park,
New Delhi - 110 017, India
Penguin Group (NZ), 67 Apollo Drive, Rosedale, Auckland 0632,
New Zealand (a division of Pearson New Zealand Ltd.)
Penguin Books (South Africa) (Pty.) Ltd., 24 Sturdee Avenue,
Rosebank, Johannesburg 2196, South Africa

Penguin Books Ltd., Registered Offices:
80 Strand, London WC2R 0RL, England

Published by Signet Classics, an imprint of New American Library,
a division of Penguin Group (USA) Inc.

First Signet Classics Printing, March 1985
First Signet Classics Printing (Bruhl and Gamer Afterword), February 2012
20 19 18 17 16

Contents

Introduction

A brief chronology of the life of Oscar Fingal O'Flahertie Wills Wilde (1854–1900) is appended to this Introduction: at the outset it is enough to say that by April of 1895 this Dublin-born writer had captivated the English-speaking world with his conversation, his lectures, his novel (*The Picture of Dorian Gray*), and his plays, two of which were running with great success in theaters in the West End of London. But his involvement with Lord Alfred Douglas (familiarly known as Bosie) and his subsequent conviction in April of 1895 for homosexual offenses with several young men of low social position effectively brought his career to an end. After his release from prison—the term was for two years—he wrote only one significant work, a long poem entitled *The Ballad of Reading Gaol*.

As early as 1881 he had encapsulated his entire career in a sonnet entitled "Hélas," which served as an epigraph to his *Poems,* Wilde's first significant book. Glancing at the echoes of Milton, Shelley, and others in this volume, *Punch* said, "The poet is Wilde, but his poetry's tame," and it must be admitted that there is something schoolboyish in calling the epigraph "Hélas" rather than "Alas"; but the poem is wise beyond its years in its perception of the consequences of rejecting "ancient wisdom and austere self-control" in favor of a life subject to "all winds."

To drift with every passion till my soul
Is a stringed lute on which all winds can play,
Is it for this that I have given away
Mine ancient wisdom, and austere control?

• • •

Surely there was a time I might have trod
The sunlit heights, and from life's dissonance
Struck one clear chord to reach the ears of God:
Is that time dead? lo! with a little rod
I did but touch the honey of romance—
And must I lose a soul's inheritance?

The sigh of the title and the note of self-criticism at the beginning are moderated in the last two-and-half lines, where Wilde, quoting 1 Samuel 14:27 (Jonathan's confession that he has broken the fast imposed upon him by Saul), insists that his offense was slight and his punishment disproportionate. With hindsight one inevitably sees in the reference to the honey-tipped rod a phallic suggestion, but the passage must, of course, more generally be taken as concerned with the conflict between Christian asceticism and what Walter Horatio Pater (1839–94)—quoting this line of the Bible in *Studies in the History of the Renaissance*—spoke of as "the artistic life, with its inevitable sensuousness." We will shortly return to Pater's *Renaissance*, which Wilde read in his first months at Oxford and which he characterized as a book that had "such a strange influence over my life," but it is worth mentioning here that Wilde as a playwright—especially as the author of *Salomé*—was also influenced by Pater's *Appreciations* (1889), in which he read that a play "attains artistic perfection just in proportion as it approaches that unity of lyrical effect, as if a song or a ballad were still lying at the root of it." With Pater's assertion of the primacy of lyric over dramatic writing, compare a remark in a letter Wilde wrote shortly after being released from Reading Gaol:

If I were asked of myself as a dramatist, I would say that my unique position was that I had taken the Drama, the most objective form known to art, and made it as personal a mode of expression as the Lyric or the Sonnet, while enriching the characterization of the stage, and enlarging—at any rate in the case of *Salome*—its artistic horizon.... The recurring phrases of *Salome,* that bind it together like a piece of music with recurring *motifs,* are, and were to me, the artistic equivalent of the old ballads.

Wilde wrote *Salomé* in French, chiefly during a stay in Paris in the fall of 1891; he did not put the final touches on it until December of that year, after he had already completed *Lady Windermere's Fan,* but we can nevertheless begin with *Salomé* in our effort to see what he contributed to "enlarging" the "horizon" of drama. There is no reason to doubt his assertion that he discussed the subject of *Salomé* at lunch with André Gide and several other French writers and, warming to his own conversation, returned to his lodgings, wrote for several hours, supped, and then finished his draft of the play. In time he submitted a French text to Pierre Louÿs and to other French writers for revision, but their contributions apparently were slight; we have Gide's word that Wilde's French was excellent. In the spring of 1892 Sarah Bernhardt was in London and asked Wilde to read the play to her. After hearing it, she told him she wanted to act the title role, and the play went into rehearsal. Public productions of plays in England, however, had to be licensed by the Lord Chamberlain, and *Salomé* was refused a license because it violated the centuries-old prohibition against portraying Biblical characters, a prohibition originating in puritan opposition to the old Roman Catholic mystery plays. (Not until 1968 was this statute removed, though it had ceased to be enforced several decades earlier.) The production of *Salomé* was therefore dropped, but the play was published in France in 1893; in 1894 it was published in an anonymous English translation, dedicated to Alfred Douglas, with a cover design and ten illustrations by Aubrey Beardsley. *Salomé* was first produced in February 1896, in France, when Wilde was still in prison. A Berlin production of 1902 was an enormous success, as was Richard Strauss's operatic version, first performed in Dresden in 1905, and it is the opera rather than either the French play or the English translation that chiefly survives on the stage. The authorship of the English translation, by the way, is uncertain. Douglas prepared a version, but Wilde was dissatisfied with it; perhaps the anonymous version—which is often said to be by Douglas—is by Wilde himself, or is Wilde's revision of Douglas's attempt. (Henceforth, because I am talking about the translation, I will use not the French but the English spelling of the name.)

No reader or viewer today is likely to be shocked by the mere fact that a Biblical episode is dramatized, but Wilde did indeed add to the story a shocking episode: Wilde's Salom kisses the decapitated head of Jokanaan (John the Baptist). There is nothing of this in the Biblical sources, Matthew and Mark, or even in any of the later written versions, such as those by Flaubert, Huysmans, Heine, and Laforgue. In most of these versions, Salome (who is not even named in the Gospels) is a minor figure, the tool of her mother, Herodias. It is Herodias who orders Salome to ask for the head of John (he had denounced Herodias because after the death of her husband she had married her brother-in-law, Herod) and—in some versions—it is Herodias who kisses the head. Only in Wilde's version does Salome kill John out of frustrated love and then kiss the decapitated head. J. K. Huysmans, however, in *À Rebours* (*Against the Grain*, 1884), had called attention to the sketchiness of the figure in the Gospels and suggested that she could be understood only by "brains shakened and sharpened,

made visionary as it were by hysteria." According to
the central figure of Huysmans's book, only the painter
Gustave Moreau had "realized" Salome, had revealed
her as "a monstrous Beast of the Apocalypse, indifferent, irresponsible, insensible, poisoning . . . all who came
near her, all who see her, all who touch her." Wilde's
sustained interest in perversity, or monstrosity, or crimi-
nality can scarcely be traced to any specific beginning,
but he surely found in *À Rebours* some confirmation of
this interest.

It is worth looking very briefly at a few of Wilde's
remarks about the relation of crime to art. In an essay
entitled "Pen, Pencil and Poison" (1889), about a man
who poisoned several people, Wilde suggests that an artist of genius is scarcely subject to our ethical judgments.
In *The Picture of Dorian Gray* (1891) an aristocrat remarks that "crime" is to the lower classes "what art is
to us, simply a method of procuring sensations." And
one can turn to a letter, undated but probably of 1885 or
1886, in which Wilde says:

> I myself would sacrifice everything for a new experi-
> ence, and I know there is no such thing as a new ex-
> perience at all. . . . Only one thing remains infinitely
> fascinating to me, the mystery of moods. To be mas-
> ter of these moods is exquisite, to be mastered by
> them more exquisite still. . . . There is an unknown
> land full of strange flowers and subtle perfumes, a
> land of which it is joy of all joys to dream, a land
> where all things are perfect and poisonous.

Or this, from an essay entitled "The Critic as Artist"
(1891):

> People sometimes say that fiction is getting too mor-
> bid. As far as psychology is concerned, it has never
> been morbid enough. We have merely touched the

surface of the soul, that is all. In one single ivory cell of the brain there are stored away things more marvellous and more terrible than even they have dreamed of who, like the author of *Le Rouge et Le Noir,* have sought to track the soul into its most secret places, and to make life confess its dearest sins.

These, and many other comments, relate Wilde to the hundred-year-old romantic tradition of men who, in Samuel Taylor Coleridge's words, "venture at times into the twilight realms of consciousness, and . . . feel a deep interest in modes of inmost being," but the writer who especially influenced Wilde was Walter Horatio Pater, and it is therefore Pater to whom we should briefly return.

Of Pater's *Studies in the History of the Renaissance* (1873, retitled *The Renaissance: Studies in Art and Poetry* in the second edition, 1877), Wilde said, according to W. B. Yeats, "It is my golden book; I never travel anywhere without it." As we have seen, Wilde read it in his first months at Oxford, and he could hardly have missed the celebrated Conclusion, in which Pater argues that external reality, apparently so solid, so evidently there, is utterly elusive and is perceived differently by each of us—and which in fact each of us perceives differently at different moments:

At first sight, experience seems to bury us under a flood of external objects, pressing upon us with a sharp and importunate reality. . . . But when reflection begins to play upon those objects they are dissipated under its influence, . . . loosed into a group of impressions—color, odor, texture—in the mind of the observer. . . . Experience, already reduced to a group of impressions, is ringed round for each one of us by that thick wall of personality through which no real voice has ever pierced on its way to us, or from us to that which we can only conjecture to be without. Every one of those impressions is the impression of the individual in his isolation, each mind keeping as a solitary prisoner its own dream of a world.

Wilde echoes this view in many writings, for example in an essay called "The Decay of Lying" when he says, "Try as we may, we cannot get behind the appearance of things to reality," and in *De Profundis*, the long letter that he wrote to Alfred Douglas from prison in 1896:

It is in the brain that everything takes place. We know now that we do not see with the eyes or hear with the ears. They are really channels for the transmission, adequate or inadequate, of sense impressions. It is in the brain that the poppy is red, that the apple is odorous, that the skylark sings.

What has this to do with *Salome*? One notices almost immediately that the moon in this play is perceived differently by the different characters. For Herodias's page, the moon (in the second speech of the play) "is like a woman rising from a tomb. She is like a dead woman." For the Young Syrian, to whom the page speaks, the moon "is like a little princess who wears a yellow veil, and whose feet are of silver. . . . One might fancy she was dancing." For Salome, the moon "is like a little piece of money, you would think she was a little silver flower." For Herod, the moon "is like a mad woman, a mad woman who is seeking everywhere for lovers." But for Herod's wife, Herodias, "the moon is like the moon, that is all." Similarly, when Salome sees Jokanaan, she says:

Thy body is white like the lilies of a field that the mower hath never mowed. Thy body is white like the snows that lie on the mountains, like the snows that lie on the mountains of Judæa, and come down into the valleys,

but a moment later, after Jokanaan rebuffs her, she says:

Thy body is hideous. It is like the body of a leper. It is like a plastered wall where vipers have crawled; like a plastered wall where the scorpions have made their nest. It is like a whitened sepulchre full of loathsome things.

In *Salome,* and especially when we are in Salome's mind, we are in the "unknown land ... where all things are perfect and poisonous," the land of the mysterious brain in which "everything takes place."

The style, or styles, that Wilde uses in *Salome* might in part be described by a passage from *Dorian Gray,* where Wilde comments on Huysmans's *À Rebours,* which he characterizes as "a psychological study of a certain young Parisian, who spent his life trying to realize in the nineteenth century all the passions and modes of thought that belonged to every century except his own. ... One hardly knew at times whether one was reading the spiritual ecstasies of some medieval saint or the morbid confessions of a modern sinner." Huysmans's style, Wilde says, consists of "elaborate paraphrases" and "subtle monotony," terms that can be applied to much of *Salome.* More exactly, in *Salome* Wilde often uses a style that is supposed to remind us of the Bible, with its repetitions, its lack of subordination, its unusual metaphors, and its catalogs. Here, for instance, is a passage from the Old Testament:

Every valley shall be exalted, and every mountain and hill shall be made low: and the crooked shall be made straight, and the rough places plain.

And here is Wilde's Jokanaan, prophesying the coming of Christ:

> When he cometh, the solitary places shall be glad. They shall blossom like the rose. The eyes of the blind shall see the day, and the ears of the deaf shall be opened. The suckling child shall put his hand upon the dragon's lair, he shall lead the lions by their manes.

The real function of this style, however, is not merely to imitate the Bible but to isolate the characters. Often the characters seem to be captivated by their own sentences, compelled to go on and on, and, surrounded by Pater's "thick wall of personality," they often seem curiously unaware of other characters, "each mind [to quote Pater again] keeping as a solitary prisoner its own dream world." The opening passage, which we have already glanced at, in which the Young Syrian and the Page of Herodias comment on the moon is only the first of many examples:

> THE YOUNG SYRIAN. How beautiful is the Princess Salomé to-night.
>
> THE PAGE OF HERODIAS. Look at the moon! How strange the moon seems. She is like a woman rising from a tomb. She is like a dead woman. One might fancy she was looking for dead things.
>
> THE YOUNG SYRIAN: She has a strange look. She is like a little princess who wears a yellow veil, and whose feet are of silver. She is like a princess who has little white doves for feet. One might fancy she was dancing.

This is scarcely dialogue (an exchange of speeches) as any dramatist before the late nineteenth century conceived of dialogue. For another example of Wilde's

"Biblical" style we can look at part of one of Salome's speeches to Jokanaan:

> It is thy mouth that I desire, Jokanaan. Thy mouth is like a band of scarlet on a tower of ivory. It is like a pomegranate cut in twain with a knife of ivory. The pomegranate-flowers that blossom in the gardens of Tyre, and are redder than roses, are not so red. The red blasts of trumpets that herald the approach of kings, and make afraid the enemy, are not so red. Thy mouth is redder than the feet of the doves who inhabit the temples . . .

The tower of ivory, the pomegranates, the blast of trumpets, the roses, the kings, and the temple, remind us of passages in the Bible; but even more important for Wilde's purpose is the sense, conveyed by this style, that, as in Pater's thought, Salome's varying perceptions or sensations of Jokanaan are all that she can know of Jokanaan. There is also in this passage an incantatory quality (we remember Wilde's pride in "the recurring phrases of *Salome,* that bind it together like a piece of music with recurring *motifs*"), which Wilde felt moved the drama toward music, in accordance with Pater's dictum that "All the arts aspire to the condition of music." In *De Profundis* Wilde speaks of himself as an artist "making beautiful colored musical things such as *Salome.*" Earlier playwrights thought that they were making plays, chiefly out of plot and character. The reference to "beautiful colored . . . things" reminds us that Wilde is, of course, also much influenced by the theories of the French Symbolists, which shaped not only lyric and dramatic poetry but also painting. Thus, in 1890 the French painter Maurice Denis—who was a close friend of the actor-manager who gave *Salomé* its first public performance—wrote words that were to become famous: "Remember that a picture—before being a war horse, a nude woman, or some anecdote—is essentially a plane surface covered with colors arranged in a certain order." That is, a work of art first of all is an independent creation, not an imitation of nature. In some of Wilde's comments on art, this comes to mean that subject matter is irrelevant and that art is chiefly decoration, but often the point is that a work of art is something designed to evoke feelings (and pleasure) in the perceiver. (I will return to this idea when I discuss *The Importance of Being Earnest.*) Thus, we come back to the passages on the moon: the different perceivers are not really describing the moon as it is, but are describing and conveying to us their feelings. Only Herodias sees the moon as merely the moon, and she is obviously the most vulgar person in the play, a person without, so to speak, a personality.

Salome, somewhat in the mode of Medea, Lady Macbeth, and Phaedra, is a figure whose powerful feelings are essentially destructive; but if she is a *femme fatale,* she is, like other tragic figures, to be judged not chiefly in ethical terms or in terms of worldly success but in terms of intensity of feeling. Salome is shocking when she strips the veils from her body, but this act of revelation is a sort of prelude to a more important revelation, the revelation of her innermost being, when she fully bares her passion by kissing the severed head: "I love thee yet, Jokanaan, I love only thee." Although the comparison may sound outrageous, in a way there is a kind of analogy here with King Lear, who also strips off his clothing as his mental experience becomes more and more painful, more and more extreme, until we are left with nothing but his passion. The intensity—far more than the ethical quality—of the tragic figure's experience is what makes the figure an object of awe in the eyes of the spectator. If we take Lear as a model and remember the tribute paid to this passionate man at the end of the play ("we that are young / Shall never see so much"), we can say that the tragic figure comes curiously close to subscribing to Pater's remark in the Conclusion to *The Renaissance,* "Not the fruit of experience, but experience itself, is the end."

Herod, like Herodias, of course survives; but he is presumably a broken man, a minor tragic figure (a sort of Creon, to Salome's Antigone?) who must live with the knowledge that he has done a deed of horror. (For all of its apparent unconventionality, *Salome* embodies the basic irony of a conventional tragic plot. Characters passionately desire something—Herod desires to see Salome dance, Salome desires the head of John the Baptist—and they get what they want; but they must pay a price greater than they had imagined.) Herodias alone is triumphant in the world (she loses her daughter, but we feel that she is chiefly concerned with humiliating Herod); she is successful because she is the most trivial person in the play. If she is in some ways the most "real" person in *Salome,* she is to the artist and to the audience the least interesting. "Nothing that actually occurs," Wilde wrote in 1884, "is of the smallest importance." Given his esthetic views, Wilde might have said that no one who fails to feel intensely is of the smallest importance.

Salome was not the first of Wilde's nine plays. As early as 1880 he had written *Vera; or The Nihilists,* a tragedy about a socialist who falls in love with a young man who turns out to be the son of the Czar. Ordered to shoot him, she instead commits suicide. The young man succeeds his father, with promises of social reform, so Vera's sacrifice is justified. The play is negligible as drama, but its political implications anticipate Wilde's essay *The Soul of Man Under Socialism* (1890) and the social interests of some of the comedies. His second play, *The Duchess of Padua* (1883), in the tradition of Elizabethan and Jacobean revenge tragedy uses blank verse for the higher figures, comic prose for the lower, and all in all reads like a pastiche of Renaissance drama though it was seriously intended. But Wilde had already established himself as a literary personality, and especially as a witty speaker both at the dinner table and on the platform. His American tour, which occupied him during much of 1882, was a great success, surprising even to his agent. The idea for a tour originated with Richard D'Oyly Carte, who thought that Wilde—regarded as the symbol of Art for Art's Sake—would furnish good publicity for D'Oyly Carte's production of Gilbert and Sullivan's *Patience,* a spoof on the Aesthetic Movement. Wilde, quite willing to exploit himself and to continue the role of the dandy already established in England by George (Beau) Brummel and Benjamin Disraeli, obliged by wearing a velvet jacket, knee-breeches, and silk stockings (this garb was strictly for American consumption) and by lecturing on art and household decorations—as well as on dress reform and on the revolutionary Irish poets of 1848. His important writing begins in the late 1880s, and from 1888 to 1895 he produced most of the work for which he is remembered: stories, critical essays, a novel, *Salome,* and four witty plays—*Lady Windermere's Fan, A Woman of No Importance, An Ideal Husband,* and *The Importance of Being Earnest.* After his arrest, conviction, and imprisonment in 1895, he produced chiefly letters—including the enormously long one, *De Profundis*—and, in 1897, after his release from jail, the only poem of his that seems to have any popular reputation, *The Ballad of Reading Gaol.*

It is to the comedies that we now turn. Wilde himself turned to this form at the suggestion of a young actor-manager, George Alexander, who, impressed by the witty conversationalist, urged Wilde to write a modern comedy. It should be mentioned that although there is no merit in the view occasionally suggested that much of the "poetic" language of *Salome* is intended as a parody, a few passages in *Salome* certainly were intended to be at least faintly amusing. A single brief example: "The

Tetrarch does not care to see dead bodies save the bodies of those whom he himself has slain."

Lady Windermere's Fan, written near Lake Windermere in the fall of 1891, combines Wilde's comic gift with his interest in social issues. The play had its premier early in 1892, and though the critical reviews were mixed, it was a popular—which is to say a financial—success. The wit is evident enough even today, but the social commentary now seems so muted as to be almost invisible. We can begin with the wit. The chief epigrammatist is Lord Darlington, who says such things as "I can resist everything except temptation," "[A cynic is] a man who knows the price of everything and the value of nothing," and "Life is far too important a thing ever to talk seriously about it." Lord Darlington by no means speaks all of the epigrams, however, probably because Wilde could not resist the temptation to make the play sparkle throughout. Moreover, fairly early in the play Darlington reveals that he has feelings: he is in love with Lady Windermere and seeks to persuade her to leave her husband. This means that he is no longer entirely suited to act the role of the witty, apparently dispassionate commentator on life, and so in large measure the wit is then assigned to others, for instance to Dumby, who delights us with such lines as "The youth of the present day are quite monstrous. They have no respect for dyed hair." Although wit, especially in the form of paradoxical and apparently unfeeling utterances, is an emblem of the dandy, the dandy is not to be regarded as a mere jester. He wears the mask of indifference, but he feels keenly. Baudelaire's "Le Dandy" (1846), as well as other writings, had argued that (in Baudelaire's words) "Dandyism is not, as many unthinking people seem to suppose, an immoderate interest in personal appearance and material elegance. For the true dandy these things are only a symbol of the aristocratic superiority of his personality." And, Baudelaire again, "Dandyism is the last burst of heroism in a time of decadence." Pater's emphasis on sensation is not found in Baudelaire, but we have in both writers an emphasis on the individual, a person set apart from the trivial people who perceive the world in conventional terms. For Wilde, and for some other authors, the world is ugly and disgusting, made bearable only by a rigorous art—that is to say, by artifice. Unconventional but carefully arranged dress, like the shapely utterances of wit, is the symbol of this passion for the discipline of art. Hence we find Wilde writing, "One should either be a work of art, or wear a work of art," and "The first duty in life is to be as artificial as possible. What the second duty is no one has as yet discovered."

The emphasis on artifice, though sometimes trivialized in Wilde, has a respectable history. The gist of the idea, as found in Baudelaire's "Praise of Cosmetics," is that nature is a fallen, wicked world (a view that has a respectable Christian history), and since we are naturally wicked it follows that virtue or the good is "artificial." "Evil," he writes, "arises of itself, naturally and by predestination. Good is always the product of a creative skill." If for "creative skill" we substitute "carefully built-up civilization," even "education" or "artifice," we can see that the idea is not utterly preposterous, though Wilde liked to put it in forms that were more shocking. For instance, he wrote: "It is only the superficial qualities that last. Man's deeper nature is soon found out." And: "What art really reveals to us is Nature's lack of design, her curious crudities, her extraordinary monotony, her absolutely unfinished condition. . . . Art is our spirited protest, our gallant attempt to teach Nature her proper place." Wilde, like some others who held that art is superior to nature, made the view visible in elegant and unusual dress, and in a studied, impassive manner—hence, of course, his costume and his sometimes heartless epigrams.

But there can be no doubt that Wilde was genuinely concerned about social issues and that he saw esthetic appreciation as a way (he told his audiences during his lecture tour, when he spoke of "The English Renaissance of Art") of creating a "beautiful national life." Similarly, his reported comments to young hustlers on the beauty of naked Greek athletes probably were genuinely high-minded; indeed, his interest in these lower-class companions was partly rooted in his belief that the appreciation of beauty should not be limited to the privileged few. His remark, in the lecture on the renaissance of art in England, that "art never harms itself by keeping aloof from the social problems of the day," is sometimes taken to be a manifesto on behalf of Art for Art's Sake, but it should be understood in the context of his view that art sets a standard to which life—in this case ugly, commercial Victorian society—should aspire. Unlike those proponents of Art for Art's Sake who see art as utterly independent of daily life, in his essays Wilde often sees art as a standard, an ideal to which life must aspire. In *The Soul of Man Under Socialism* (1890), his only sustained political essay, he argues that humanity is most likely to achieve its fullest development in a classless society that has abolished private property. Only under these conditions can life be beautiful.

How much social criticism, we may ask, can one find in *Lady Windermere's Fan*? A little in the epigrams, and perhaps a little more in the overall plot. Like *A Woman of No Importance, Lady Windermere's Fan* has a woman with a guilty past (in *A Woman of No Importance* Mrs. Arbuthnot has had an illegitimate son), and the audience, along with Lady Windermere, is brought to see that such a person can be "a very good woman," to quote the final line of the play. But these "social dramas," or "social comedies," or "society comedies" can scarcely be said to challenge society's values, say as the plays of Ibsen do. (Translations of Ibsen were made in England in the 1870s, and at least half a dozen of Ibsen's plays had been performed in London by the time of *Lady Windermere*; *A Doll's House,* for instance, was performed as early as 1889.)

In *Lady Windermere's Fan,* Lady Windermere begins as a sort of puritan, strongly condemning Mrs. Erlynne, but she learns two things: that she herself is capable of performing a guilty act (leaving her husband, abandoning her child), and that the despised Mrs. Erlynne is capable of performing a self-sacrificing act. And so Lady Windermere is moved to her final judgment that Mrs. Erlynne is "a very good woman." The play might seem to merit the title "The Education of Lady Windermere," especially since the action is set, significantly, on her twenty-first birthday, the day she comes of age, but the more one thinks about it, the less satisfactory this reading is. Lady Windermere never learns that Mrs. Erlynne is her mother—a relationship that makes Mrs. Erlynne's act of self-sacrifice somewhat less disinterested. And, more important, the play never vigorously suggests that indeed a woman may be justified in abandoning her husband and child. That is, Mrs. Erlynne looks on her early action, when she left her family, as a terrible mistake, and it is clear to the audience that Lady Windermere's proposed flight from her family is similarly a mistake. After all, her daring action (luckily never completed) is based entirely on the mistaken belief that her husband is unfaithful. Lord Darlington, urging her to leave her husband, offers her his love and this encouragement:

> I won't tell you that the world matters nothing, or the world's voice, or the voice of society. They matter a good deal. They matter far too much. But there are moments when one has to choose between living one's own life, fully, entirely, completely—or dragging out some false, shallow, degrading existence

that the world in its hypocrisy demands. You have that moment now. Choose! Oh, my love, choose.

She does briefly leave her husband, taking refuge in Lord Darlington's apartment, but she is persuaded to return to her husband by Mrs. Erlynne, and since it turns out her flight to Darlington was in any case based on a misunderstanding (Lord Windermere has been constant to his wife), Lord Darlington's unorthodox views are undercut. Any resemblance to Ibsen thus soon disappears. What Shaw rightly saw as "the technical novelty" of the new, Ibsenite drama was the scene of *discussion* toward which a play moved (e.g. Nora and Torvald sitting down to talk things over near the end of *A Doll's House*), but the passage from *Lady Windermere* is spoken early in the play and the issue is never really analyzed any further. And as has been mentioned, though Lady Windermere at the end of the play takes an altogether different view from the puritanical speech quoted a moment ago, she does so in ignorance of the facts: Mrs. Erlynne's past is still a secret unknown to Lady Windermere. In this play, then, the topic of infidelity is, so to speak, flirted with but never consummated. Scandal-mongering and hypocrisy are rebuffed, and a sinner is forgiven, but none of this represents a challenge to the settled views of the audience. A play that at first may seem, especially in Lord Darlington's words, to challenge society, ends up, after some melodramatic moments, with all the usual values intact. The play never faces the question of what is the right, or even the duty, of a wife whose husband is indeed unfaithful. *Lady Windermere's Fan* thus toys with social issues, especially with the double standard in sexual morality, but it remains in large measure a comedy (with melodramatic passages) about the usual stuff of comedy, misunderstandings. Although Wilde might have been surprised to learn that his play is conventional, he would not have regarded such a judgment as calling attention to a weakness in the play, and it does not: the job of a playwright, he would have said, is to create a work of beauty, not a work of social criticism.

Here we can return to the role of the dandy held first by Lord Darlington and later by others, including (though it is not immediately obvious) Mrs. Erlynne. "Manners before morals," she coolly says to the indignant Lord Windermere, thus summarizing the apparent creed of the dandy. Mrs. Erlynne has for the most part the admirable poise of the dandy, except when her daughter's welfare is at stake, but in the last scene she outdoes herself:

> I suppose, Windermere, you would like me to retire into a convent, or become a hospital nurse, or something of that kind, as people do in silly modern novels. That is stupid of you, Arthur; in real life we don't do such things—not as long as we have any good looks left, at any rate. No—what consoles one nowadays is not repentance, but pleasure. Repentance is quite out of date. And besides, if a woman really repents, she has to go to a bad dress-maker, otherwise no one believes in her. And nothing in the world would induce me to do that. No; I am going to pass entirely out of your two lives. My coming into them has been a mistake—I discovered that last night.

Clever speech and reserved feeling here, of course, are the mask (to use a term from Wilde's critical writings) that allows her to perform what in the context of the play is the best thing to do. There is no doubt that Mrs. Erlynne is to be viewed as highly moral. "I regret my bad actions," she tells Lord Windermere, "you regret your good ones—that is the difference between us," another statement that is thoroughly dandiacal in its flippancy and in its fundamental morality.

If we judge *Lady Windermere's Fan* as though it were

a play by Ibsen, or even by Shaw, it of course seems weak, though in a few passages the play seems to invite comparison.

> LORD DARLINGTON. . . . Do you think seriously that women who have committed what the world calls a fault should never be forgiven?
>
> LADY WINDERMERE. I think they should never be forgiven.
>
> LORD DARLINGTON. And men? Do you think that there should be the same laws for men as there are for women?
>
> LADY WINDERMERE. Certainly!
>
> LORD DARLINGTON. I think life too complex a thing to be settled by these hard and fast rules.
>
> LADY WINDERMERE. If we had "these hard and fast rules" we should find life much more simple.

In *Earnest,* Algernon will say, "The truth is rarely pure and never simple." And Lady Windermere will, by the end of the play, come to see that Mrs. Erlynne—though a liar—is not simply (as Lord Windermere says) "a very clever woman" but "a very good woman." The weakness of the play is not that it fails to offer new, Ibsenite values (judged by this standard, most of Shakespeare's plays would be found wanting) but that we are asked to take seriously some unconvincing, melodramatic speeches, such as Lord Windermere's at the end of the first act, when his wife tells him that if Mrs. Erlynne enters the Windermere house she will strike Mrs. Erlynne with her fan. She strides out, and we are left with Lord Windermere:

> LORD WINDERMERE (*calling after her*). Margaret! Margaret! (*A pause.*) My God! What shall I do? I dare not tell her who this woman really is. The shame would kill her. (*Sinks down into a chair and buries his face in his hands.*)

Wilde took seriously the job of constructing a play. In his original version of *Lady Windermere's Fan* the secret—that Mrs. Erlynne is Lady Windermere's mother—was withheld until the last act. When the producer urged Wilde to let the audience in on the secret earlier, Wilde replied in a letter that to do so would "destroy the dramatic wonder" by making Mrs. Erlynne's sacrifice natural rather than unexpected. After a few performances Wilde revised the play, putting the revelation earlier, but his original version, as well as many speeches in the final version, shows that Wilde was striving for melodramatic as well as for comic effects. That is, his comedy is cast in the form of the "well-made play," the *pièce bien faite* as established by the French playwright Victorien Sardou (1831–1908), a cleverly plotted play with much suspense but little or no subtlety of characterization (the characters are more likely to be inconsistent than complex), a sort of melodrama with the fisticuffs left out. It can, in fact, be argued that *Lady Windermere's Fan* is not really to be classified as a "comedy" but as a "drama," though one with a good deal of witty dialogue.

Wilde continued to work in this genre in *A Woman of No Importance* (produced early in 1893) and *An Ideal Husband* (produced in 1895), but he abandoned it for what can be called pure comedy in *The Importance of Being Earnest* (written in 1894 and produced in 1895). For George Bernard Shaw, reviewing the first production of what was to be Wilde's last play, the piece was "rib-tickling" but lacking in "humanity." For most readers and viewers, however, *The Importance of Being Earnest* is Wilde's greatest work, the only play in which, freeing himself from melodramatic claptrap, he wrote a delightfully intricate plot (the four lovers are sometimes partners, sometimes competitors) with consistently witty dialogue. It is, so to speak, a play that is pure *play*. In *Earnest* there is, to be sure, the motif of the long-lost child that is found also in *Lady Windermere* and in *A Woman of No Importance,* but in those plays the identification was serious, whereas in *Earnest* the discovery that Jack is the long-lost Ernest, who as an infant had been absentmindedly misplaced in a handbag and left at a railroad station, is unambiguously comic. In his review Shaw conjectured that Wilde had refurbished an early work written under the influence of W. S. Gilbert, a work, Shaw said, "almost inhuman enough to have been conceived" by Gilbert. Shaw could not believe that *Earnest* represented Wilde's mature artistic achievement. Some twenty years later Shaw again commented on the play, calling it "heartless," and attributing to Wilde's "debaucheries" the lack in *Earnest* of the "kindness and gallantry" that Shaw found in Wilde's earlier plays. He did not specify any passages or episodes, but we might agree that when Jack's "I have lost both my parents" gets as its response from Lady Bracknell, "Both? ... That seems like carelessness," we are not in the realm of kindness or gallantry. And it is certainly true that whatever gallant statements occur in *Earnest* are undermined. Thus, after Miss Prism identifies the old handbag as hers, Jack exclaims, "Miss Prism, more is restored to you than this handbag. I was the baby you placed in it." He goes on to call Miss Prism "mother," and then, when she indignantly says, "Mr. Worthing, I am unmarried," he heroically responds:

> Unmarried! I do not deny that is a serious blow. But after all, who has the right to cast a stone against one who has suffered? Cannot repentance wipe out an act of folly? Why should there be one law for men, and another for women? Mother, I forgive you. (*Tries to embrace her again.*)

Out of context, a daring speech—though here not daring of course, but comic, since it is addressed to the prim Miss Prism.

What, then, is the play about, or is it about nothing? Some readers see it as a variant of Wilde's three earlier witty society dramas with their characters who try to conceal shameful secrets: they find, in this motif of a secret, a veiled allusion to Wilde's homosexuality—a sort of ambiguous confession, or, rather, an ambiguous challenge to society, since his sinners are strong figures, modern versions of Salome, who also defies society. Something has already been said of Wilde's view that the artist is a sort of brother to the criminal; to this it should be added that Wilde's taste in sex included good-looking semi-criminal types whom he romanticized. "It was like feasting with panthers," he wrote in *De Profundis*: "The danger was half the excitement." But too much can be made of the view that the plays are daring revelations of a dangerous secret. Secrets are the stuff of much drama, from *Oedipus* (Oedipus has killed his father and married his mother) to the present, and they were especially common in the well-made plays of the late nineteenth century. It is easy enough to reject this view that the play is a sinner's artful confession and thus an effort at self-exculpation, but is the play merely what Wilde said it was, something "by a butterfly for butterflies"? In his letters, where Wilde never hesitates to take his works seriously and to lecture his reader on them, none of the comments about *Earnest* suggests that the play is to be taken seriously: "The great charm of the play is in the dialogue"; "my play is really very funny"; and (as late as 1899), *Earnest* is "a fanciful absurd comedy." None of this is inconsistent with Wilde's statements, made throughout his career as a writer, that (to quote from "The Decay of Lying") "Art never expresses anything but itself," or, to quote the first lines of the Preface to *Dorian Gray,* "The artist is the creator of beautiful things." This is much of a piece with Maurice Denis's statement, already quoted, that a picture "before being a war horse, a nude woman, or some anecdote—is essentially a plane surface covered with colors arranged in a certain order." But to this it can be replied that *Earnest* is filled with talk about important matters, such as love and marriage and divorce and illegitimacy, education, class relationships, appearance and reality, and death. How seriously does the play allow us to take these themes? Wilde subtitled the play "A Trivial Comedy for Serious People," and he told a friend that the play has a "philosophy." What was this philosophy? Wilde explained: "We should treat all the trivial things of life seriously, and all the serious things of life with sincere and studied triviality." This is, of course, again the language of the dandy, designed to shock—but also, perhaps, to stimulate thought and to induce a new perspective.

Perhaps the play is about exactly what its title announces, the importance of being earnest—even in play. Algernon says to Jack, "I happen to be serious about Bunburying. What you are serious about I haven't got the remotest idea. About everything, I should fancy. You have an absolutely trivial nature." Algernon is mistaken in his view of Jack, but the point here, reinforced by the title and by the end of the play, is that one must find something to be serious about, i.e. one must not live a mechanical, conventional life but must (in Pater's words in the Conclusion to *The Renaissance*) burn with a "hard, gemlike flame." In the earlier witty plays Wilde tried, at least in some passages, to be serious about the world around him, but this task (dare one say it?) was too much for him. *The Soul of Man Under Socialism,* where Wilde writes as a polemicist rather than as an artist, too clearly shows that Wilde was not in any reasonable definition of the term a profound thinker about matters other than the arts. In *Earnest,* however, he determined at last to be serious only about comedy, and he wrote a masterpiece. Perhaps, then, we can accept Shaw's view that the play is inhuman without accepting his evaluation that it is therefore unworthy. (Elsewhere Shaw made amends of a sort, saying that he picked up his "passion for fun from Oscar Wilde.") Again we are reminded of Pater's Conclusion, where, after characterizing "success in life" as the ability to burn with a gemlike flame, an ability to get "as many pulsations into life as possible," Pater says: "Art comes to you proposing frankly to give nothing but the highest quality to your moments as they pass, and simply for those moments' sake." Salome burned with a gemlike flame, and presumably the play about her is supposed to induce in the spectator a similar intensity. In *Earnest*, Gwendolyn provides us with a delightful comic version: "This suspense is terrible. I hope it will last." Substitute Shaw's "rib-tickling" for Gwendolyn's "suspense," and we get an intensity that surely Pater did not have in mind but that nonetheless has established the play among the great comedies of the world.

A final, bibliographical point: Wilde drafted *Earnest* in four acts, but was persuaded by the producer to reduce it to three. Acts II and III were combined to form the present Act III, chiefly by the omission of an episode concerning one Gribsby, which we print as an appendix. The omission of this episode from the final version of the play is a real loss, but it should be pointed out that the four-act version is essentially a draft—it lacks much of the wit of the later, three-act version—and cannot by any means be regarded as the play that Wilde would have put on the stage if it had not been for the interference of the producer. The three-act version is the version that he approved for production and later (with the addition of small improvements in the dialogue) for publication. When in 1898 he prepared *The Importance of Being Earnest* for publication, he knew that the stage version was far in advance of his earlier, four-act draft. For instance, in the manuscript (four-act) version Algernon's "Now produce your explanation, and pray make it remarkable" is followed by these rather dead sentences: "The bore about most explanations is that they are never half so remarkable as the things they try to explain. That is why modern science is so absolutely tedious." This passage appears also in the typescript of the three-act version, but it is crossed out there. Wilde continued to revise, even on the proofs he received from the publisher, and so in the published version we get something much more concise and much better: "Now produce your explanation, and pray make it improbable." To regard the four-act version as authoritative, then, is to reject Wilde's many improvements. But the loss of Gribsby is regrettable, and we therefore print the episode beginning on page 181.

—SYLVAN BARNET
Tufts University

Chronology

Salomé

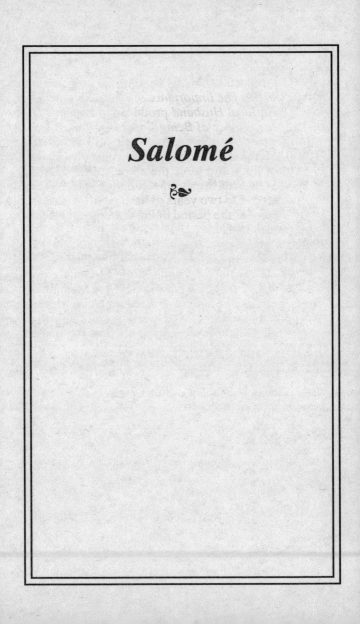

CHARACTERS

HEROD ANTIPAS (*Tetrarch of Judæa*)

JOKANAAN (*The Prophet*)

THE YOUNG SYRIAN (*Captain of the Guard*)

TIGELLINUS (*A Young Roman*)

A CAPPADOCIAN

A NUBIAN

FIRST SOLDIER

SECOND SOLDIER

THE PAGE OF HERODIAS

JEWS, NAZARENES, ETC.

A SLAVE

NAAMAN (*The Executioner*)

HERODIAS (*Wife of the Tetrarch*)

SALOMÉ (*Daughter of Herodias*)

THE SLAVES OF SALOMÉ

SCENE.—*A great terrace in the Palace of* HEROD, *set above the banqueting-hall. Some soldiers are leaning over the balcony. To the right there is a gigantic staircase, to the left, at the back, an old cistern surrounded by a wall of green bronze. The moon is shining very brightly.*

THE YOUNG SYRIAN. How beautiful is the Princess Salomé to-night!

THE PAGE OF HERODIAS. Look at the moon. How strange the moon seems! She is like a woman rising from a tomb. She is like a dead woman. One might fancy she was looking for dead things.

THE YOUNG SYRIAN. She has a strange look. She is like a little princess who wears a yellow veil, and whose feet are of silver. She is like a princess who has little white doves for feet. One might fancy she was dancing.

THE PAGE OF HERODIAS. She is like a woman who is dead. She moves very slowly. (*Noise in the banqueting-hall.*)

FIRST SOLDIER. What an uproar! Who are those wild beasts howling?

SECOND SOLDIER. The Jews. They are always like that. They are disputing about their religion.

FIRST SOLDIER. Why do they dispute about their religion?

3

SECOND SOLDIER. I cannot tell. They are always doing it. The Pharisees, for instance, say that there are angels, and the Sadducees declare that angels do not exist.

FIRST SOLDIER. I think it is ridiculous to dispute about such things.

THE YOUNG SYRIAN. How beautiful is the Princess Salomé to-night!

THE PAGE OF HERODIAS. You are always looking at her. You look at her too much. It is dangerous to look at people in such fashion. Something terrible may happen.

THE YOUNG SYRIAN. She is very beautiful to-night.

FIRST SOLDIER. The Tetrarch has a sombre aspect.

SECOND SOLDIER. Yes; he has a sombre aspect.

FIRST SOLDIER. He is looking at something.

SECOND SOLDIER. He is looking at some one.

FIRST SOLDIER. At whom is he looking?

SECOND SOLDIER. I cannot tell.

THE YOUNG SYRIAN. How pale the Princess is! Never have I seen her so pale. She is like the shadow of a white rose in a mirror of silver.

THE PAGE OF HERODIAS. You must not look at her. You look too much at her.

FIRST SOLDIER. Herodias has filled the cup of the Tetrarch.

THE CAPPADOCIAN. Is that the Queen Herodias, she who wears a black mitre sewed with pearls, and whose hair is powdered with blue dust?

FIRST SOLDIER. Yes; that is Herodias, the Tetrarch's wife.

SECOND SOLDIER. The Tetrarch is very fond of wine. He has wine of three sorts. One which is brought from the Island of Samothrace, and is purple like the cloak of Cæsar.

THE CAPPADOCIAN. I have never seen Cæsar.

SECOND SOLDIER. Another that comes from a town called Cyprus, and is as yellow as gold.

THE CAPPADOCIAN. I love gold.

SECOND SOLDIER. And the third is a wine of Sicily. That wine is red as blood.

THE NUBIAN. The gods of my country are very fond of blood. Twice in the year we sacrifice to them young men and maidens; fifty young men and a hundred maidens. But I am afraid that we never give them quite enough, for they are very harsh to us.

THE CAPPADOCIAN. In my country there are no gods left. The Romans have driven them out. There are some who say that they have hidden themselves in the mountains, but I do not believe it. Three nights I have been on the mountains seeking them everywhere. I did not find them. And at last I called them by their names, and they did not come. I think they are dead.

FIRST SOLDIER. The Jews worship a God that one cannot see.

THE CAPPADOCIAN. I cannot understand that.

FIRST SOLDIER. In fact, they only believe in things that one cannot see.

THE CAPPADOCIAN. That seems to me altogether ridiculous.

THE VOICE OF JOKANAAN. After me shall come another mightier than I. I am not worthy so much as to unloose the latchet of his shoes. When he cometh, the solitary places shall be glad. They shall blossom like the rose. The eyes of the blind shall see the day, and the ears of the deaf shall be opened. The suckling child shall put his hand upon the dragon's lair, he shall lead the lions by their manes.

SECOND SOLDIER. Make him be silent. He is always saying ridiculous things.

FIRST SOLDIER. No, no. He is a holy man. He is very gentle, too. Every day, when I give him to eat he thanks me.

THE CAPPADOCIAN. Who is he?

FIRST SOLDIER. A prophet.

THE CAPPADOCIAN. What is his name?

FIRST SOLDIER. Jokanaan.

THE CAPPADOCIAN. Whence comes he?

FIRST SOLDIER. From the desert where he fed on locusts and wild honey. He was clothed in camel's hair, and round his loins he had a leathern belt. He was very terrible to look upon. A great multitude used to follow him. He even had disciples.

THE CAPPADOCIAN. What is he talking of?

FIRST SOLDIER. We can never tell. Sometimes he says things that affright one, but it is impossible to understand what he says.

THE CAPPADOCIAN. May one see him?

FIRST SOLDIER. No. The Tetrarch has forbidden it.

THE YOUNG SYRIAN. The Princess has hidden her face behind her fan! Her little white hands are fluttering like doves that fly to their dovecotes. They are like white butterflies. They are just like white butterflies.

THE PAGE OF HERODIAS. What is that to you? Why do you look at her? You must not look at her.... Something terrible may happen.

THE CAPPADOCIAN (*pointing to the cistern*). What a strange prison!

SECOND SOLDIER. It is an old cistern.

THE CAPPADOCIAN. An old cistern! That must be a poisonous place in which to dwell!

SECOND SOLDIER. Oh, no! For instance, the Tetrarch's brother, his elder brother, the first husband of Herodias the Queen, was imprisoned there for twelve years. It did not kill him. At the end of the twelve years he had to be strangled.

THE CAPPADOCIAN. Strangled? Who dared to do that?

SECOND SOLDIER (*pointing to the Executioner, a huge Negro*). That man yonder, Naaman.

THE CAPPADOCIAN. He was not afraid?

SECOND SOLDIER. Oh, no! The Tetrarch sent him the ring.

THE CAPPADOCIAN. What ring?

SECOND SOLDIER. The death-ring. So he was not afraid.

THE CAPPADOCIAN. Yet it is a terrible thing to strangle a king.

FIRST SOLDIER. Why? Kings have but one neck, like other folk.

THE CAPPADOCIAN. I think it terrible.

THE YOUNG SYRIAN. The Princess is getting up! She is leaving the table! She looks very troubled. Ah, she is coming this way. Yes, she is coming towards us. How pale she is! Never have I seen her so pale.

THE PAGE OF HERODIAS. I pray you not to look at her.

THE YOUNG SYRIAN. She is like a dove that has strayed.... She is like a narcissus trembling in the wind.... She is like a silver flower.

(*Enter* SALOMÉ.)

SALOMÉ. I will not stay. I cannot stay. Why does the Tetrarch look at me all the while with his mole's eyes under his shaking eyelids? It is strange that the husband of my mother looks at me like that. I know not what it means. Of a truth I know it too well.

THE YOUNG SYRIAN. You have left the feast, Princess?

SALOMÉ. How sweet is the air here! I can breathe here! Within there are Jews from Jerusalem who are tearing each other in pieces over their foolish ceremonies, and barbarians who drink and drink, and spill their wine on the pavement, and Greeks from Smyrna with painted eyes and painted cheeks, and frizzed hair curled in columns, and Egyptians silent and subtle, with long nails of jade and russet cloaks, and Romans brutal and coarse, with their uncouth jargon. Ah! how I loathe the Romans! They are rough and common, and they give themselves the airs of noble lords.

THE YOUNG SYRIAN. Will you be seated, Princess?

THE PAGE OF HERODIAS. Why do you speak to her? Oh! something terrible will happen. Why do you look at her?

SALOMÉ. How good to see the moon! She is like a little piece of money, a little silver flower. She is cold and chaste. I am sure she is a virgin. Yes, she is a virgin. She has never defiled herself. She has never abandoned herself to men, like the other goddesses.

THE VOICE OF JOKANAAN. Behold! the Lord hath come. The Son of Man is at hand. The centaurs have hidden themselves in the rivers, and the nymphs have left the rivers, and are lying beneath the leaves of the forest.

SALOMÉ. Who was that who cried out?

SECOND SOLDIER. The prophet, Princess.

SALOMÉ. Ah, the prophet! He of whom the Tetrarch is afraid?

SECOND SOLDIER. We know nothing of that, Princess. It was the prophet Jokanaan who cried out.

THE YOUNG SYRIAN. Is it your pleasure that I bid them bring your litter, Princess? The night is fair in the garden.

SALOMÉ. He says terrible things about my mother, does he not?

SECOND SOLDIER. We never understand what he says, Princess.

SALOMÉ. Yes; he says terrible things about her.

(*Enter a Slave.*)

THE SLAVE. Princess, the Tetrarch prays you to return to the feast.

THE YOUNG SYRIAN. Pardon me, Princess, but if you return not some misfortune may happen.

SALOMÉ. Is he an old man, this prophet?

THE YOUNG SYRIAN. Princess, it were better to return. Suffer me to lead you in.

SALOMÉ. This prophet . . . is he an old man?

FIRST SOLDIER. No, Princess, he is quite young.

SECOND SOLDIER. One cannot be sure. There are those who say he is Elias.

SALOMÉ. Who is Elias?

SECOND SOLDIER. A prophet of this country in bygone days, Princess.

THE SLAVE. What answer may I give the Tetrarch from the Princess?

THE VOICE OF JOKANAAN. Rejoice not, O Land of Palestine, because the rod of him who smote thee is broken. For from the seed of the serpent shall come a basilisk, and that which is born of it shall devour the birds.

SALOMÉ. What a strange voice! I would speak with him.

FIRST SOLDIER. I fear it may not be, Princess. The Tetrarch does not suffer any one to speak with him. He has even forbidden the high priest to speak with him.

SALOMÉ. I desire to speak with him.

FIRST SOLDIER. It is impossible, Princess.

THE YOUNG SYRIAN. Would it not be better to return to the banquet?

SALOMÉ. Bring forth this prophet. (*Exit the Slave.*)

FIRST SOLDIER. We dare not, Princess.

SALOMÉ (*approaching the cistern and looking down into it*). How black it is, down there! It must be terrible to be in so black a hole! It is like a tomb. . . . (*To the SOLDIERS.*) Did you not hear me? Bring out the prophet. I would look on him.

SECOND SOLDIER. Princess, I beg you, do not require this of us.

SALOMÉ. You are making me wait upon your pleasure.

FIRST SOLDIER. Princess, our lives belong to you, but we cannot do what you have asked of us. And indeed, it is not of us that you should ask this thing.

SALOMÉ (*looking at* THE YOUNG SYRIAN). Ah!

THE PAGE OF HERODIAS. Oh! what is going to happen? I am sure that something terrible will happen.

SALOMÉ (*going up to* THE YOUNG SYRIAN). Thou wilt do this thing for me, wilt thou not, Narraboth? Thou wilt do this thing for me. I have ever been kind towards thee. Thou wilt do it for me. I would but look at him, this strange prophet. Men have talked so much of him. Often I have heard the Tetrarch talk of him. I think he is afraid of him, the Tetrarch. Art thou, even thou, also afraid of him, Narraboth?

THE YOUNG SYRIAN. I fear him not, Princess; there is no man I fear. But the Tetrarch has formally forbidden that any man should raise the cover of this well.

SALOMÉ. Thou wilt do this thing for me, Narraboth, and to-morrow when I pass in my litter beneath the gateway of the idol-sellers I will let fall for thee a little flower, a little green flower.

THE YOUNG SYRIAN. Princess, I cannot, I cannot.

SALOMÉ (smiling). Thou wilt do this thing for me, Narraboth. Thou knowest that thou wilt do this thing for me. And on the morrow when I pass in my litter by the bridge of the idol-buyers, I will look at thee through the muslin veils, I will look at thee, Narraboth, it may be I will smile at thee. Look at me, Narraboth, look at me. Ah! thou knowest that thou wilt do what I ask of thee. Thou knowest it. . . . I know that thou wilt do this thing.

THE YOUNG SYRIAN (signing to the THIRD SOLDIER). Let the prophet come forth. . . . The Princess Salomé desires to see him.

SALOMÉ. Ah!

THE PAGE OF HERODIAS. Oh! How strange the moon looks. Like the hand of a dead woman who is seeking to cover herself with a shroud.

THE YOUNG SYRIAN. She has a strange aspect! She is like a little princess, whose eyes are eyes of amber. Through the clouds of muslin she is smiling like a little princess. (The prophet comes out of the cistern. SALOMÉ looks at him and steps slowly back.)

JOKANAAN. Where is he whose cup of abominations is now full? Where is he, who in a robe of silver shall one day die in the face of all the people? Bid him come forth, that he may hear the voice of him who hath cried in the waste places and in the houses of kings.

SALOMÉ. Of whom is he speaking?

THE YOUNG SYRIAN. No one can tell, Princess.

JOKANAAN. Where is she who saw the images of men painted on the walls, even the images of the Chaldeans painted with colours, and gave herself up unto the lust of her eyes, and sent ambassadors into the land of Chaldea?

SALOMÉ. It is of my mother that he is speaking?

THE YOUNG SYRIAN. Oh, no, Princess.

SALOMÉ. Yes; it is of my mother that he is speaking.

JOKANAAN. Where is she who gave herself unto the Captains of Assyria, who have baldricks on their loins, and crowns of many colours on their heads? Where is she who hath given herself to the young men of the Egyptians, who are clothed in fine linen and hyacinth, whose shields are of gold, whose helmets are of silver, whose bodies are mighty? Go bid her rise up from the bed of her abominations, from the bed of her incestuousness, that she may hear the words of him who prepareth the way of the Lord, that she may repent her of her iniquities. Though she will not repent, but will stick fast in her abominations; go, bid her come, for the fan of the Lord is in His hand.

SALOMÉ. Ah, but he is terrible, he is terrible!

THE YOUNG SYRIAN. Do not stay here, Princess, I beseech you.

SALOMÉ. It is his eyes above all that are terrible. They are like black holes burned by torches in a tapestry of Tyre. They are like the black caverns of Egypt in which the dragons make their lairs. They are like black lakes troubled by fantastic moons. . . . Do you think he will speak again?

THE YOUNG SYRIAN. Do not stay here, Princess. I pray you, do not stay here.

SALOMÉ. How wasted he is! He is like a thin ivory statue. He is like an image of silver. I am sure he is chaste as the moon is. He is like a moonbeam, like a shaft of silver. I would look closer at him. I must look at him closer.

THE YOUNG SYRIAN. Princess! Princess!

JOKANAAN. Who is this woman who is looking at me? I will not have her look at me. Wherefore doth she look at me with her golden eyes, under her gilded eyelids? I know not who she is. I do not desire to know who she is. Bid her begone. It is not to her that I would speak.

SALOMÉ. I am Salomé, daughter of Herodias, Princess of Judæa.

JOKANAAN. Back! daughter of Babylon! Come not near the chosen of the Lord. Thy mother hath filled the earth with the wine of her iniquities, and the cry of her sinning hath come up even to the ears of God.

SALOMÉ. Speak again, Jokanaan. Thy voice is as music to mine ear.

THE YOUNG SYRIAN. Princess! Princess! Princess!

SALOMÉ. Speak again! Speak again, Jokanaan, and tell me what I must do.

JOKANAAN. Daughter of Sodom, come not near me! But cover thy face with a veil, and scatter ashes upon thine head, and get thee to the desert and seek out the Son of Man.

SALOMÉ. Who is he, the Son of Man? Is he as beautiful as thou art, Jokanaan?

JOKANAAN. Get thee behind me! I hear in the palace the beating of the wings of the angel of death.

THE YOUNG SYRIAN. Princess, I beseech thee to go within.

JOKANAAN. Angel of the Lord God, what dost thou here with thy sword? Whom seekest thou in this palace? The day of him who shall die in a robe of silver has not yet come.

SALOMÉ. Jokanaan!

JOKANAAN. Who speaketh?

SALOMÉ. I am amorous of thy body, Jokanaan! Thy body is white like the lilies of a field that the mower

hath never mowed. Thy body is white like the snows
that lie on the mountains of Judæa, and come down
into the valleys. The roses in the garden of the Queen of
Arabia are not so white as thy body. Neither the roses
of the garden of the Queen of Arabia, the garden of
spices of the Queen of Arabia, nor the feet of the dawn
when they light on the leaves, nor the breast of the
moon when she lies on the breast of the sea. . . . There
is nothing in the world so white as thy body. Suffer me
to touch thy body.

JOKANAAN. Back! daughter of Babylon! By woman
came evil into the world. Speak not to me. I will not listen to thee. I listen but to the voice of the Lord God.

SALOMÉ. Thy body is hideous. It is like the body of
a leper. It is like a plastered wall where vipers have
crawled; like a plastered wall where the scorpions have
made their nest. It is like a whitened sepulchre full of
loathsome things. It is horrible, thy body is horrible. It is
thy hair that I am enamoured of, Jokanaan. Thy hair is
like clusters of grapes, like the clusters of black grapes
that hang from the vine-trees of Edom in the land of
the Edomites. Thy hair is like the cedars of Lebanon,
like the great cedars of Lebanon that give their shade
to the lions and to the robbers who would hide them
by day. The long black nights, when the moon hides her
face, when the stars are afraid, are not so black as thy
hair. The silence that dwells in the forest is not so black.
There is nothing in the world that is so black as thy
hair. . . . Suffer me to touch thy hair.

JOKANAAN. Back, daughter of Sodom! Touch me not.
Profane not the temple of the Lord God.

SALOMÉ. Thy hair is horrible. It is covered with mire
and dust. It is like a knot of serpents coiled round thy
neck. I love not thy hair. . . . It is thy mouth that I desire,
Jokanaan. Thy mouth is like a band of scarlet on a tower
of ivory. It is like a pomegranate cut in twain with a
knife of ivory. The pomegranate-flowers that blossom in

the gardens of Tyre, and are redder than roses, are not so red. The red blasts of trumpets that herald the approach of kings, and make afraid the enemy, are not so red. Thy mouth is redder than the feet of the doves who inhabit the temples and are fed by the priest. It is redder than the feet of him who cometh from a forest where he hath slain a lion, and seen gilded tigers. Thy mouth is like a branch of coral that fishers have found in the twilight of the sea, the coral that they keep for the kings! ... It is like the vermilion that the Moabites find in the mines of Moab, the vermilion that the kings take from them. It is like the bow of the King of the Persians, that is painted with vermilion, and is tipped with coral. There is nothing in the world so red as thy mouth.... Suffer me to kiss thy mouth.

JOKANAAN. Never! daughter of Babylon! Daughter of Sodom! Never.

SALOMÉ. I will kiss thy mouth, Jokanaan. I will kiss thy mouth.

THE YOUNG SYRIAN. Princess, Princess, thou art like a garden of myrrh, thou who art the dove of all doves, look not at this man, look not at him! Do not speak such words to him. I cannot endure it.... Princess, do not speak these things.

SALOMÉ. I will kiss thy mouth, Jokanaan.

THE YOUNG SYRIAN. Ah! (*He kills himself and falls between* SALOMÉ *and* JOKANAAN.)

THE PAGE OF HERODIAS. The young Syrian has slain himself! The young captain has slain himself! He has slain himself who was my friend! I gave him a little box of perfumes and ear-rings wrought in silver, and now he has killed himself! Ah, did he not say that some misfortune would happen? I, too, said it, and it has come to pass. Well I knew that the moon was seeking a dead thing, but I knew not that it was he whom she sought. Ah! why did I not hide him from the moon? If I had hidden him in a cavern she would not have seen him.

FIRST SOLDIER. Princess, the young captain has just slain himself.

SALOMÉ. Suffer me to kiss thy mouth, Jokanaan.

JOKANAAN. Art thou not afraid, daughter of Herodias? Did I not tell thee that I had heard in the palace the beating of the wings of the angel of death, and hath he not come, the angel of death?

SALOMÉ. Suffer me to kiss thy mouth.

JOKANAAN. Daughter of adultery, there is but one who can save thee, it is He of whom I spake. Go seek Him. He is in a boat on the sea of Galilee, and He talketh with His disciples. Kneel down on the shore of the sea, and call unto Him by His name. When He cometh to thee (and to all who call on Him He cometh), bow thyself at His feet and ask of Him the remission of thy sins.

SALOMÉ. Suffer me to kiss thy mouth.

JOKANAAN. Cursed be thou! daughter of an incestuous mother, be thou accursed!

SALOMÉ. I will kiss thy mouth, Jokanaan.

JOKANAAN. I will not look at thee, thou art accursed, Salomé, thou art accursed. (*He goes down into the cistern.*)

SALOMÉ. I will kiss thy mouth, Jokanaan; I will kiss thy mouth.

FIRST SOLDIER. We must bear away the body to another place. The Tetrarch does not care to see dead bodies, save the bodies of those whom he himself has slain.

THE PAGE OF HERODIAS. He was my brother, and nearer to me than a brother. I gave him a little box full of perfumes, and a ring of agate that he wore always on his hand. In the evening we were wont to walk by the river, and among the almond trees, and he used to tell me of the things of his country. He spake ever very low. The sound of his voice was like the sound of the flute, of one who playeth upon the flute. Also he had much joy to gaze at himself in the river. I used to reproach him for that.

SECOND SOLDIER. You are right; we must hide the body. The Tetrarch must not see it.

FIRST SOLDIER. The Tetrarch will not come to this place. He never comes on the terrace. He is too much afraid of the prophet.

(*Enter* HEROD, HERODIAS, *and all the Court.*)

HEROD. Where is Salomé? Where is the Princess? Why did she not return to the banquet as I commanded her? Ah! There she is!

HERODIAS. You must not look at her! You are always looking at her!

HEROD. The moon has a strange look to-night. Has she not a strange look? She is like a mad woman who is seeking everywhere for lovers. She is naked, too. She is quite naked. The clouds are seeking to clothe her nakedness, but she will not let them. She shows herself naked in the sky. She reels through the clouds like a drunken woman....I am sure she is looking for lovers. Does she not reel like a drunken woman? She is like a mad woman, is she not?

HERODIAS. No; the moon is like the moon, that is all. Let us go within.... We have nothing to do here.

HEROD. I will stay here! Manasseh, lay carpets there. Light torches, bring forth the ivory table, and the tables of jasper. The air here is sweet. I will drink more wine with my guests. We must show all honours to the ambassadors of Cæsar.

HERODIAS. It is not because of them that you remain.

HEROD. Yes; the air is very sweet. Come, Herodias, our guests await us. Ah! I have slipped! I have slipped in blood! It is an ill omen. Wherefore is there blood here? ... and this body, what does this body here? Think you I am like the King of Egypt, who gives no feast to his guests but that he shows them a corpse? Whose is it? I will not look on it.

FIRST SOLDIER. It is our captain, sire. He is the young Syrian whom you made captain of the guard but three days gone.

HEROD. I issued no order that he should be slain.

SECOND SOLDIER. He slew himself, sire.

HEROD. For what reason? I had made him captain of my guard.

SECOND SOLDIER. We do not know, sire. But with his own hand he slew himself.

HEROD. That seems strange to me. I had thought it was but the Roman philosophers who slew themselves. Is it not true, Tigellinus, that the philosophers at Rome slay themselves?

TIGELLINUS. There may be some who slay themselves, sire. They are the Stoics. The Stoics are people of no cultivation. They are ridiculous people. I myself regard them as being perfectly ridiculous.

HEROD. I also. It is ridiculous to kill oneself.

TIGELLINUS. Everybody at Rome laughs at them. The Emperor has written a satire against them. It is recited everywhere.

HEROD. Ah! he has written a satire against them? Cæsar is wonderful. He can do everything.... It is strange that the young Syrian has slain himself. I am sorry he has slain himself. I am very sorry, for he was fair to look upon. He was even very fair. He had very languorous eyes. I remember that I saw that he looked languorously at Salomé. Truly, I thought he looked too much at her.

HERODIAS. There are others who look too much at her.

HEROD. His father was a king. I drove him from his kingdom. And of his mother, who was a queen, you made a slave—Herodias. So he was here as my guest, as it were, and for that reason I made him my captain. I am sorry he is dead. Ho! why have you left the body here? I will not look at it—away with it! (*They take away the body*.) It is cold here. There is a wind blowing. Is there not a wind blowing?

HERODIAS. No; there is no wind.

HEROD. I tell you there is a wind that blows. . . . And I hear in the air something that is like the beating of wings, like the beating of vast wings. Do you not hear it?

HERODIAS. I hear nothing.

HEROD. I hear it no longer. But I heard it. It was the blowing of the wind. It has passed away. But no, I hear it again. Do you not hear it? It is just like the beating of wings.

HERODIAS. I tell you there is nothing. You are ill. Let us go within.

HEROD. I am not ill. It is your daughter who is sick to death. Never have I seen her so pale.

HERODIAS. I have told you not to look at her.

HEROD. Pour me forth wine. (*Wine is brought.*) Salomé, come drink a little wine with me. I have here a wine that is exquisite. Cæsar himself sent it me. Dip into it thy little red lips, that I may drain the cup.

SALOMÉ. I am not thirsty, Tetrarch.

HEROD. You hear how she answers me, this daughter of yours?

HERODIAS. She does right. Why are you always gazing at her?

HEROD. Bring me ripe fruits. (*Fruits are brought.*) Salomé, come and eat fruits with me. I love to see in a fruit the mark of thy little teeth. Bite but a little of this fruit that I may eat what is left.

SALOMÉ. I am not hungry, Tetrarch.

HEROD (*to* HERODIAS). You see how you have brought up this daughter of yours.

HERODIAS. My daughter and I come of a royal race. As for thee, thy father was a camel driver! He was a thief and a robber to boot!

HEROD. Thou liest!

HERODIAS. Thou knowest well that it is true.

HEROD. Salomé, come and sit next to me. I will give thee the throne of thy mother.

SALOMÉ. I am not tired, Tetrarch.

HERODIAS. You see in what regard she holds you.

HEROD. Bring me—what is it that I desire? I forget. Ah! ah! I remember.

THE VOICE OF JOKANAAN. Behold, the time is come! That which I foretold has come to pass. The day that I spoke of is at hand.

HERODIAS. Bid him be silent. I will not listen to his voice. This man is for ever hurling insults against me.

HEROD. He has said nothing against you. Besides, he is a very great prophet.

HERODIAS. I do not believe in prophets. Can a man tell what will come to pass? No man knows it. Also he is for ever insulting me. But I think you are afraid of him. . . . I know well that you are afraid of him.

HEROD. I am not afraid of him. I am afraid of no man.

HERODIAS. I tell you, you are afraid of him. If you are not afraid of him why do you not deliver him to the Jews who for these six months past have been clamouring for him?

A JEW. Truly, my lord, it were better to deliver him into our hands.

HEROD. Enough on this subject. I have already given you my answer. I will not deliver him into your hands. He is a holy man. He is a man who has seen God.

A JEW. That cannot be. There is no man who hath seen God since the prophet Elias. He is the last man who saw God face to face. In these days God doth not show Himself. God hideth Himself. Therefore great evils have come upon the land.

ANOTHER JEW. Verily, no man knoweth if Elias the prophet did indeed see God. Peradventure it was but the shadow of God that he saw.

A THIRD JEW. God is at no time hidden. He showeth

Himself at all times and in all places. God is in what is evil even as He is in what is good.

A FOURTH JEW. Thou shouldst not say that. It is a very dangerous doctrine. It is a doctrine that cometh from Alexandria, where men teach the philosophy of the Greeks. And the Greeks are Gentiles. They are not even circumcised.

A FIFTH JEW. No one can tell how God worketh. His ways are very dark. It may be that the things which we call evil are good, and that the things which we call good are evil. There is no knowledge of any thing. We can but bow our heads to His will, for God is very strong. He breaketh in pieces the strong together with the weak, for He regardeth not any man.

FIRST JEW. Thou speakest truly. Verily God is terrible. He breaketh in pieces the strong and the weak as a man breaks corn in a mortar. But as for man, he hath never seen God. No man hath seen God since the prophet Elias.

HERODIAS. Make them be silent. They weary me.

HEROD. But I have heard it said that Jokanaan is in very truth your prophet Elias.

THE JEW. That cannot be. It is more than three hundred years since the days of the prophet Elias.

HEROD. There be some who say that this man is Elias the prophet.

A NAZARENE. I am sure that he is Elias the prophet.

THE JEW. Nay, but he is not Elias the prophet.

THE VOICE OF JOKANAAN. Behold, the day is at hand, the day of the Lord, and I heard upon the mountains the feet of Him who shall be the Saviour of the world.

HEROD. What does that mean? The Saviour of the world?

TIGELLINUS. It is a title that Cæsar adopts.

HEROD. But Cæsar is not coming into Judæa. Only yesterday I received letters from Rome. They contained nothing concerning this matter. And you, Tigellinus, who were at Rome during the winter, you heard nothing concerning this matter, did you?

TIGELLINUS. Sire, I heard nothing concerning the matter. I was explaining the title. It is one of Cæsar's titles.

HEROD. But Cæsar cannot come. He is too gouty. They say that his feet are like the feet of an elephant. Also there are reasons of State. He who leaves Rome loses Rome. He will not come. Howbeit, Cæsar is lord, he will come if such be his pleasure. Nevertheless, I think he will not come.

FIRST NAZARENE. It was not concerning Cæsar that the prophet spake these words, sire.

HEROD. How?—it was not concerning Cæsar?

FIRST NAZARENE. No, my lord.

HEROD. Concerning whom then did he speak?

FIRST NAZARENE. Concerning the Messiah who has come.

A JEW. The Messiah hath not come.

FIRST NAZARENE. He hath come, and everywhere He worketh miracles.

HERODIAS. Ho! ho! miracles! I do not believe in miracles. I have seen too many. (*To the* PAGE.) My fan.

FIRST NAZARENE. This Man worketh true miracles. Thus, at a marriage which took place in a little town of Galilee, a town of some importance, He changed water into wine. Certain persons who were present related it to me. Also He healed two lepers that were seated before the Gate of Capernaum simply by touching them.

SECOND NAZARENE. Nay; it was blind men that He healed at Capernaum.

FIRST NAZARENE. Nay; they were lepers. But He hath healed blind people also, and He was seen on a mountain talking with angels.

A SADDUCEE. Angels do not exist.

A PHARISEE. Angels exist, but I do not believe that this Man has talked with them.

FIRST NAZARENE. He was seen by a great multitude of people talking with angels.

HERODIAS. How these men worry me! They are ridiculous! (*To the* PAGE.) Well! my fan! (*The* PAGE *gives her the fan.*) You have a dreamer's look; you must not dream. It is only sick people who dream. (*She strikes the* PAGE *with her fan.*)

SECOND NAZARENE. There is also the miracle of the daughter of Jairus.

FIRST NAZARENE. Yea, that is sure. No man can gainsay it.

HERODIAS. These men are mad. They have looked too long on the moon. Command them to be silent.

HEROD. What is this miracle of the daughter of Jairus?

FIRST NAZARENE. The daughter of Jairus was dead. This Man raised her from the dead.

HEROD. How! He raises people from the dead?

FIRST NAZARENE. Yea, sire, He raiseth the dead.

HEROD. I do not wish Him to do that. I forbid Him to do that. I suffer no man to raise the dead. This Man must be found and told that I forbid Him to raise the dead. Where is this Man at present?

SECOND NAZARENE. He is in every place, my lord, but it is hard to find Him.

FIRST NAZARENE. It is said that He is now in Samaria.

A JEW. It is easy to see that this is not the Messiah, if He is in Samaria. It is not to the Samaritans that the Messiah shall come. The Samaritans are accursed. They bring no offerings to the Temple.

SECOND NAZARENE. He left Samaria a few days since. I think that at the present moment He is in the neighbourhood of Jerusalem.

FIRST NAZARENE. No; he is not there. I have just come from Jerusalem. For two months they have had no tidings of Him.

HEROD. No matter! But let them find Him, and tell Him, thus saith Herod the King, "I will not suffer Thee to raise the dead!" To change water into wine, to heal the lepers and the blind. . . . He may do these things if He will. I say nothing against these things. In truth I hold it a kindly deed to heal a leper. But no man shall raise the dead. It would be terrible if the dead came back.

THE VOICE OF JOKANAAN. Ah! the wanton one! The harlot! Ah! the daughter of Babylon with her golden eyes and her gilded eyelids! Thus saith the Lord God, Let there come up against her a multitude of men. Let the people take stones and stone her. . . .

HERODIAS. Command him to be silent.

THE VOICE OF JOKANAAN. Let the captains of the hosts pierce her with their swords, let them crush her beneath their shields.

HERODIAS. Nay, but it is infamous.

THE VOICE OF JOKANAAN. It is thus that I will wipe out all wickedness from the earth, and that all women shall learn not to imitate her abominations.

HERODIAS. You hear what he says against me? You suffer him to revile her who is your wife?

HEROD. He did not speak your name.

HERODIAS. What does that matter? You know well that it is I whom he seeks to revile. And I am your wife, am I not?

HEROD. Of a truth, dear and noble Herodias, you are my wife, and before that you were the wife of my brother.

HERODIAS. It was thou didst snatch me from his arms.

HEROD. Of a truth I was stronger than he was. . . . But let us not talk of that matter. I do not desire to talk of it. It is the cause of the terrible words that the prophet has spoken. Peradventure on account of it a misfortune will come. Let us not speak of this matter. Noble Herodias, we are not mindful of our guests. Fill thou my cup, my well-beloved. Ho! fill with wine the great goblets of silver, and the great goblets of glass. I will drink to Cæsar. There are Romans here, we must drink to Cæsar.

ALL. Cæsar! Cæsar!

HEROD. Do you not see your daughter, how pale she is?

HERODIAS. What is that to you if she be pale or not?

HEROD. Never have I seen her so pale.

HERODIAS. You must not look at her.

THE VOICE OF JOKANAAN. In that day the sun shall become black like sackcloth of hair, and the moon shall become like blood, and the stars of the heavens shall fall upon the earth like unripe figs that fall from the fig-tree, and the kings of the earth shall be afraid.

HERODIAS. Ah! Ah! I should like to see that day of which he speaks, when the moon shall become like blood, and when the stars shall fall upon the earth like unripe figs. This prophet talks like a drunken man . . . but I cannot suffer the sound of his voice. I hate his voice. Command him to be silent.

HEROD. I will not. I cannot understand what it is that he saith, but it may be an omen.

HERODIAS. I do not believe in omens. He speaks like a drunken man.

HEROD. It may be he is drunk with the wine of God.

HERODIAS. What wine is that, the wine of God? From what vineyards is it gathered? In what wine-press may one find it?

HEROD (*from this point he looks all the while at* SA-LOMÉ). Tigellinus, when you were at Rome of late, did the Emperor speak with you on the subject of . . . ?

TIGELLINUS. On what subject, my lord?

HEROD. On what subject? Ah! I asked you a question, did I not? I have forgotten what I would have asked you.

HERODIAS. You are looking again at my daughter. You must not look at her. I have already said so.

HEROD. You say nothing else.

HERODIAS. I say it again.

HEROD. And that restoration of the Temple about which they have talked so much, will anything be done?

They say the veil of the sanctuary has disappeared, do they not?

HERODIAS. It was thyself didst steal it. Thou speakest at random and without wit. I will not stay here. Let us go within.

HEROD. Dance for me, Salomé.

HERODIAS. I will not have her dance.

SALOMÉ. I have no desire to dance, Tetrarch.

HEROD. Salomé, daughter of Herodias, dance for me.

HERODIAS. Peace! let her alone.

HEROD. I command thee to dance, Salomé.

SALOMÉ. I will not dance, Tetrarch.

HERODIAS (*laughing*). You see how she obeys you.

HEROD. What is it to me whether she dance or not? It is naught to me. To-night I am happy, I am exceeding happy. Never have I been so happy.

FIRST SOLDIER. The Tetrarch has a sombre look. Has he not a sombre look?

SECOND SOLDIER. Yes, he has a sombre look.

HEROD. Wherefore should I not be happy? Cæsar, who is lord of the world, Cæsar, who is lord of all things, loves me well. He has just sent me most precious gifts. Also he has promised me to summon to Rome the King of Cappadocia, who is my enemy. It may be that at Rome he will crucify him, for he is able to do all things that he has a mind to. Verily, Cæsar is lord. Therefore I do well to be happy. There is nothing in the world that can mar my happiness.

THE VOICE OF JOKANAAN. He shall be seated on his throne. He shall be clothed in scarlet and purple. In his hand he shall bear a golden cup full of his blasphemies. And the angel of the Lord shall smite him. He shall be eaten of worms.

HERODIAS. You hear what he says about you. He says that you will be eaten of worms.

HEROD. It is not of me that he speaks. He speaks never against me. It is of the King of Cappadocia that he speaks; the King of Cappadocia who is mine enemy. It is he who shall be eaten of worms. It is not I. Never has he spoken word against me, this prophet, save that I sinned in taking to wife the wife of my brother. It may be he is right. For, of a truth, you are sterile.

HERODIAS. I am sterile, I? You say that, you that are ever looking at my daughter, you that would have her dance for your pleasure? You speak as a fool. I have borne a child. You have gotten no child, no, not on one of your slaves. It is you who are sterile, not I.

HEROD. Peace, woman! I say that you are sterile. You have borne me no child, and the prophet says that our marriage is not a true marriage. He says that it is a marriage of incest, a marriage that will bring evils. . . . I fear he is right; I am sure that he is right. I would be happy at this. Of a truth, I am happy. There is nothing I lack.

HERODIAS. I am glad you are of so fair a humour to-night. It is not your custom. But it is late. Let us go within. Do not forget that we hunt at sunrise. All honours must be shown to Cæsar's ambassadors, must they not?

SECOND SOLDIER. The Tetrarch has a sombre look.

FIRST SOLDIER. Yes, he has a sombre look.

HEROD. Salomé, Salomé, dance for me. I pray thee dance for me. I am sad to-night. Yes; I am passing sad to-night. When I came hither I slipped in blood, which is an evil omen; also I heard in the air a beating of wings, a beating of giant wings. I cannot tell what they mean. . . . I am sad to-night. Therefore dance for me. Dance for me, Salomé, I beseech thee. If thou dancest for me thou mayest ask of me what thou wilt, and I will give it thee, even unto the half of my kingdom.

SALOMÉ (*rising*). Will you indeed give me whatsoever I shall ask of thee, Tetrarch?

HERODIAS. Do not dance, my daughter.

HEROD. Whatsoever thou shalt ask of me, even unto the half of my kingdom.

SALOMÉ. You swear it, Tetrarch?

HEROD. I swear it, Salomé.

HERODIAS. Do not dance, my daughter.

SALOMÉ. By what will you swear this thing, Tetrarch?

HEROD. By my life, by my crown, by my gods. Whatsoever thou shalt desire I will give it thee, even to the half of my kingdom, if thou wilt but dance for me. O Salomé, Salomé, dance for me!

SALOMÉ. You have sworn an oath, Tetrarch.

HEROD. I have sworn an oath.

HERODIAS. My daughter, do not dance.

HEROD. Even to the half of my kingdom. Thou wilt be passing fair as a queen, Salomé, if it please thee to ask for half of my kingdom. Will she not be fair as a queen? Ah! it is cold here! There is an icy wind, and I hear... wherefore do I hear in the air this beating of wings? Ah! one might fancy a huge black bird that hovers over the terrace. Why can I not see it, this bird? The beat of its wings is terrible. The breath of the wind of its wings is terrible. It is a chill wind. Nay, but it is not cold, it is hot. I am choking. Pour water on my hands. Give me snow to eat. Loosen my mantle. Quick! quick! loosen my mantle. Nay, but leave it. It is my garland that hurts me, my garland of roses. The flowers are like fire. They have burned my forehead. (*He tears the wreath from his head and throws it on the table.*) Ah! I can breathe now. How red those petals are! They are like stains of blood on the cloth. That does not matter. It is not wise to find symbols in everything that one sees. It makes life too full of terrors. It were better to say that stains of blood are as lovely as rose petals. It were better far to say that. . . . But we will not speak of this. Now I am happy. I am passing happy. Have I not the right to be happy? Your daughter is going to dance for me. Wilt thou not dance for me, Salomé? Thou hast promised to dance for me.

HERODIAS. I will not have her dance.

SALOMÉ. I will dance for you, Tetrarch.

HEROD. You hear what your daughter says. She is going to dance for me. Thou doest well to dance for me, Salomé. And when thou hast danced for me, forget not to ask of me whatsoever thou hast a mind to ask. Whatsoever thou shalt desire I will give it thee, even to the half of my kingdom. I have sworn it, have I not?

SALOMÉ. Thou hast sworn it, Tetrarch.

HEROD. And I have never broken my word. I am not of those who break their oaths. I know not how to lie. I am the slave of my word, and my word is the word of a king. The King of Cappadocia had ever a lying tongue, but he is no true king. He is a coward. Also he owes me money that he will not repay. He has even insulted my ambassadors. He has spoken words that were wounding. But Cæsar will crucify him when he comes to Rome. I know that Cæsar will crucify him. And if he crucify him not, yet will he die, being eaten of worms. The prophet has prophesied it. Well! wherefore dost thou tarry, Salomé?

SALOMÉ. I am waiting until my slaves bring perfumes to me and the seven veils, and take from off my feet my sandals. (*Slaves bring perfumes and the seven veils, and take off the sandals of* SALOMÉ.)

HEROD. Ah, thou art to dance with naked feet. 'Tis well! 'Tis well. Thy little feet will be like white doves. They will be like little white flowers that dance upon the trees. . . . No, no, she is going to dance on blood. There is blood spilt on the ground. She must not dance on blood. It were an evil omen.

HERODIAS. What is it to thee if she dance on blood? Thou hast waded deep enough in it. . . .

HEROD. What is it to me? Ah! look at the moon! She has become red. She has become red as blood. Ah! the prophet prophesied truly. He prophesied that the moon would become as blood. Did he not prophesy it? All of ye heard him prophesying it. And now the moon has become as blood. Do ye not see it?

HERODIAS. Oh, yes, I see it well, and the stars are falling like unripe figs, are they not? and the sun is becoming black like sackcloth of hair, and the kings of the earth are afraid. That at least one can see. The prophet is justified of his words in that at least, for truly the kings of the earth are afraid. . . . Let us go within. You are sick. They will say at Rome that you are mad. Let us go within, I tell you.

THE VOICE OF JOKANAAN. Who is this who cometh from Edom, who is this who cometh from Bozra, whose raiment is dyed with purple, who shineth in the beauty of his garments, who walketh mighty in his greatness? Wherefore is thy raiment stained with scarlet?

HERODIAS. Let us go within. The voice of that man maddens me. I will not have my daughter dance while he is continually crying out. I will not have her dance while you look at her in this fashion. In a word, I will not have her dance.

HEROD. Do not rise, my wife, my queen, it will avail thee nothing. I will not go within till she hath danced. Dance, Salomé, dance for me.

HERODIAS. Do not dance, my daughter.

SALOMÉ. I am ready, Tetrarch. (SALOMÉ *dances the dance of the seven veils.*)

HEROD. Ah! wonderful! wonderful! You see that she has danced for me, your daughter. Come near, Salomé, come near, that I may give thee thy fee. Ah! I pay a royal price to those who dance for my pleasure. I will pay thee royally. I will give thee whatsoever thy soul desireth. What wouldst thou have? Speak.

SALOMÉ (*kneeling*). I would that they presently bring me in a silver charger . . .

HEROD (*laughing*). In a silver charger? Surely yes, in a silver charger. She is charming, is she not? What is it thou wouldst have in a silver charger, O sweet and fair Salomé, thou that art fairer than all the daughters of Judæa? What wouldst thou have them bring thee in a silver charger? Tell me. Whatsoever it may be, thou shalt receive it. My treasures belong to thee. What is it that thou wouldst have, Salomé?

SALOMÉ (*rising*). The head of Jokanaan.

HERODIAS. Ah! that is well said, my daughter.

HEROD. No, no!

HERODIAS. That is well said, my daughter.

HEROD. No, no, Salomé. It is not that thou desirest. Do not listen to thy mother's voice. She is ever giving thee evil council. Do not heed her.

SALOMÉ. It is not my mother's voice that I heed. It is for mine own pleasure that I ask the head of Jokanaan in a silver charger. You have sworn an oath, Herod. Forget not that you have sworn an oath.

HEROD. I know it. I have sworn an oath by my gods. I know it well. But I pray thee, Salomé, ask of me something else. Ask of me the half of my kingdom, and I will give it thee. But ask not of me what thy lips have asked.

SALOMÉ. I ask of you the head of Jokanaan.

HEROD. No, no, I will not give it thee.

SALOMÉ. You have sworn an oath, Herod.

HERODIAS. Yes, you have sworn an oath. Everybody heard you. You swore it before everybody.

HEROD. Peace, woman! It is not to you I speak.

HERODIAS. My daughter has done well to ask the head of Jokanaan. He has covered me with insults. He has said unspeakable things against me. One can see that she loves her mother well. Do not yield, my daughter. He has sworn an oath, he has sworn an oath.

HEROD. Peace! Speak not to me! ... Salomé, I pray thee be not stubborn. I have ever been kind towards thee. I have ever loved thee.... It may be that I have loved thee too much. Therefore ask not this thing of me. This is a terrible thing, an awful thing to ask of me. Surely, I think thou art jesting. The head of a man that is cut from his body is ill to look upon, is it not? It is not meet that the eyes of a virgin should look upon such a thing. What pleasure couldst thou have in it? There is no pleasure that thou couldst have in it. No, no, it is not that thou desirest. Hearken to me. I have an emerald, a great emerald, thou canst see that which passeth afar off. Cæsar himself carries such an emerald when he goes to the circus. But my emerald is the larger. I know well that it is the larger. It is the largest emerald in the whole world. Thou wilt take that, wilt thou not? Ask it of me, and I will give it thee.

SALOMÉ. I demand the head of Jokanaan.

HEROD. Thou art not listening. Thou art not listening. Suffer me to speak, Salomé.

SALOMÉ. The head of Jokanaan.

HEROD. No, no, thou wouldst not have that. Thou sayest that but to trouble me, because I have looked at thee and ceased not this night. It is true, I have looked at thee and ceased not this night. Thy beauty has troubled me. Thy beauty has grievously troubled me, and I have looked at thee over-much. Nay, but I will look at thee no more. One should not look at anything. Neither at things, nor at people should one look. Only in mirrors is it well to look, for mirrors do but show us masks. Oh! oh! bring wine! I thirst.... Salomé, Salomé, let us be as friends. Bethink thee.... Ah! what would I say? What was't? Ah! I remember it! ... Salomé—nay, but come nearer to me; I fear thou wilt not hear my words—Salomé, thou knowest my white peacocks, my beautiful white peacocks, that walk in the garden between the myrtles and the tall cypress trees. Their beaks are gilded with gold and the grains that they eat are smeared with gold, and their feet are stained with purple. When they cry out the rain comes, and the moon shows herself in the heavens when they spread their tails. Two by two they walk between the cypress trees and the black myrtles, and each has a slave to tend it. Sometimes they fly across the trees, and anon they crouch in the grass, and round the pools of the water. There are not in all the world birds so wonderful. I know that Cæsar himself has no birds so fair as my birds. I will give thee fifty of my peacocks. They will follow thee whithersoever thou goest, and in the midst of them thou wilt be like unto the moon in the midst of a great white cloud. . . . I will give them to thee all. I have but a hundred, and in the whole world there is no king who has peacocks like unto my peacocks. But I will give them all to thee. Only thou must loose me from my oath, and must not ask of me that which thy lips have asked of me. (*He empties the cup of wine.*)

SALOMÉ. Give me the head of Jokanaan.

HERODIAS. Well said, my daughter! As for you, you are ridiculous with your peacocks.

HEROD. Ah! thou art not listening to me. Be calm. As for me, am I not calm? I am altogether calm. Listen. I have jewels hidden in this palace—jewels that thy mother even has never seen; jewels that are marvellous to look at. I have a collar of pearls, set in four rows. They are like unto moons chained with rays of silver. They are even as half a hundred moons caught in a golden net. On the ivory breast of a queen they have rested. Thou shalt be as fair as a queen when thou wearest them. I have amethysts of two kinds, one that is black like wine, and one that is red like wine that one has coloured with water. I have topazes, yellow as are the eyes of tigers, and topazes that are pink as the eyes of a wood-pigeon, and green topazes that are as the eyes of cats. I have opals that burn always, with a flame that is cold as ice, opals that make sad men's minds, and are afraid of the shadows. I have onyxes like the eyeballs of a dead woman. I have moonstones that change when the moon changes, and are wan when they see the sun. I have sapphires big like eggs, and as blue as blue flowers. The sea wanders within them and the moon comes never to trouble the blue of their waves. I have chrysolites and beryls and chrysoprases and rubies. I have sardonyx and hyacinth stones, and stones of chalcedony, and I will give them all unto thee, all, and other things will I add to them. The

King of the Indies has but even now sent me four fans fashioned from the feathers of parrots, and the King of Numidia a garment of ostrich feathers. I have a crystal, into which it is not lawful for a woman to look, nor may young men behold it until they have been beaten with rods. In a coffer of nacre I have three wondrous turquoises. He who wears them on his forehead can imagine things which are not, and he who carries them in his hand can turn the fruitful woman into a woman that is barren. These are great treasures above all price. But this is not all. In an ebony coffer I have two cups, amber, that are like apples of pure gold. If an enemy pour poison into these cups they become like apples of silver. In a coffer incrusted with amber I have sandals incrusted with glass. I have mantles that have been brought from the land of the Seres, and bracelets decked about with carbuncles and with jade that comes from the city of Euphrates. . . . What desirest thou more than this, Salomé! Tell me the thing that thou desirest, and I will give it thee. All that thou askest I will give thee, save one thing only. I will give thee all that is mine, save only the head of one man. I will give thee the mantle of the high priest. I will give thee the veil of the sanctuary.

THE JEWS. Oh! oh!

SALOMÉ. Give me the head of Jokanaan.

HEROD (*sinking back in his seat*). Let her be given what she asks! Of a truth she is her mother's child! (*The FIRST SOLDIER approaches.* HERODIAS *draws from the hand of the Tetrarch the ring of death, and gives it to the Soldier, who straightway bears it to the Executioner. The Executioner looks scared.*) Who has taken my ring? There was a ring on my right hand. Who has drunk my wine? There was wine in my cup. It was full of wine. Someone has drunk it! Oh! surely some evil will befall some one. (*The Executioner goes down into the cistern.*) Ah! Wherefore did I give my oath? Hereafter, let no king swear an oath. If he keep it not, it is terrible, and if he keep it, it is terrible also.

HERODIAS. My daughter has done well.

HEROD. I am sure that some misfortune will happen.

SALOMÉ (*she leans over the cistern and listens*). There is no sound. I hear nothing. Why does he not cry out, this man? Ah! if any man sought to kill me, I would cry out, I would struggle, I would not suffer.... Strike, strike, Naaman, strike, I tell you.... No, I hear nothing. There is a silence, a terrible silence. Ah! something has fallen upon the ground. I heard something fall. He is afraid, this slave. He is a coward, this slave! Let soldiers be sent. (*She sees the* PAGE OF HERODIAS *and addresses him.*) Come hither; thou wert the friend of him who is dead, wert thou not? Well, I tell thee, there are not dead men enough. Go to the soldiers and bid them go down and bring me the thing I ask, the thing the Tetrarch has promised me, the thing that is mine. (*The* PAGE *recoils. She turns to the* SOLDIERS.) Hither, ye soldiers. Get ye down into this cistern and bring me the head of this man. Tetrarch, Tetrarch, command your soldiers that they bring me the head of Jokanaan. (*A huge black arm, the arm of the Executioner, comes forth from the cistern, bearing on a silver shield the head of* JOKANAAN. SALOMÉ *seizes it.* HEROD *hides his face with his cloak.* HERODIAS *smiles and fans herself. The* NAZARENES *fall on their knees and begin to pray.*) Ah! thou wouldst not suffer me to kiss thy mouth, Jokanaan. Well, I will kiss it now. I will bite it with my teeth as one bites a ripe fruit. Yes, I will kiss thy mouth, Jokanaan. I said it; did I not say it? I said it. Ah! I will kiss it now.... But, wherefore dost thou not look at me, Jokanaan? Thine eyes that were so terrible, so full of rage and scorn, are shut now. Wherefore are they shut? Open thine eyes! Lift up thine eyelids, Jokanaan! Wherefore dost thou not look at me? Art thou afraid of me, Jokanaan, that thou wilt not look at me? ... And thy tongue, that was like a red snake darting poison, it moves no more, it speaks no words,

Jokanaan, that scarlet viper that spat its venom upon me. It is strange, is it not? How is it that the red viper stirs no longer? . . . Thou wouldst have none of me, Jokanaan. Thou rejectedst me. Thou didst speak evil words against me. Thou didst bear thyself toward me as to a harlot, as to a woman that is a wanton, to me, Salomé, daughter of Herodias, Princess of Judæa! Well, I still live, but thou art dead, and thy head belongs to me. I can do with it what I will. I can throw it to the dogs and to the birds of the air. That which the dogs leave, the birds of the air shall devour. . . . Ah, Jokanaan, thou wert the man that I loved alone among men. All other men were hateful to me. But thou wert beautiful! Thy body was a column of ivory set upon feet of silver. It was a garden full of doves and lilies of silver. It was a tower of silver decked with shields of ivory. There was nothing in the world so white as thy body. There was nothing in the world so black as thy hair. In the whole world there was nothing so red as thy mouth. Thy voice was a censer that scattered strange perfumes, and when I looked on thee I heard a strange music. Ah! wherefore didst thou not look at me, Jokanaan? With the cloak of thine hands and with the cloak of thy blasphemies thou didst hide thy face. Thou didst put upon thine eyes the covering of him who would see his God. Well, thou hast seen thy God, Jokanaan, but me, me, thou didst never see. If thou hadst seen me thou hadst loved me. I saw thee, and I loved thee. Oh, how I loved thee! I love thee yet, Jokanaan, I love only thee. . . . I am athirst for thy beauty; I am hungry for thy body; and neither wine nor apples can appease my desire. What shall I do now, Jokanaan? Neither the floods nor the great waters can quench my passion. I was a princess, and thou didst scorn me. I was a virgin, and thou didst take my virginity from me. I was chaste, and thou didst fill my veins with fire. . . . Ah! ah! wherefore didst thou not look at me? If thou hadst looked at

me thou hadst loved me. Well I know that thou wouldst
have loved me, and the mystery of love is greater than
the mystery of death.

HEROD. She is monstrous, thy daughter. I tell thee she
is monstrous. In truth, what she has done is a great crime.
I am sure that it is. A crime against some unknown God.

HERODIAS. I am well pleased with my daughter. She
has done well. And I would stay here now.

HEROD (*rising*). Ah! There speaks my brother's wife!
Come! I will not stay in this place. Come, I tell thee.
Surely some terrible thing will befall. Manasseh, Issa-
dar, Zias, put out the torches. I will not look at things, I
will not suffer things to look at me. Put out the torches!
Hide the moon! Hide the stars! Let us hide ourselves in
our palace, Herodias. I begin to be afraid. (*The slaves put
out the torches. The stars disappear. A great cloud crosses
the moon and conceals it completely. The stage becomes
quite dark. The Tetrarch begins to climb the staircase.*)

THE VOICE OF SALOMÉ. Ah! I have kissed thy mouth,
Jokanaan, I have kissed thy mouth. There was a bitter
taste on my lips. Was it the taste of blood? . . . Nay; but
perchance it was the taste of love. . . . They say that love
hath a bitter taste. . . . But what matter? What matter? I
have kissed thy mouth.

HEROD (*turning round and seeing* SALOMÉ). Kill that
woman! (*The soldiers rush forward and crush beneath
their shields* SALOMÉ, *daughter of* HERODIAS, *Princess of
Judæa.*)

CURTAIN

Lady Windermere's Fan

CHARACTERS

LORD WINDERMERE	THE DUCHESS OF BERWICK
LORD DARLINGTON	LADY AGATHA CARLISLE
LORD AUGUSTUS LORTON	LADY PLYMDALE
MR. CECIL GRAHAM	LADY JEDBURGH
MR. DUMBY	LADY STUTFIELD
MR. HOPPER	MRS. COWPER-COWPER
PARKER (*Butler*)	MRS. ERLYNNE
LADY WINDERMERE	ROSALIE (*Maid*)

THE SCENES OF THE PLAY

ACT I. Morning-room in Lord Windermere's house.
ACT II. Drawing-room in Lord Windermere's house.
ACT III. Lord Darlington's rooms.
ACT IV. Same as Act I.

TIME.—The Present. PLACE.—London.

The action of the play takes place within twenty-four hours, beginning on a Tuesday afternoon at five o'clock and ending the next day at 1:30 p.m.

ACT I

SCENE.—*Morning-room of* LORD WINDERMERE's *house in Carlton House Terrace. Doors* C. *and* R. *Bureau with books and papers* R. *Sofa with small tea-table* L. *Window opening on to terrace* L. *Table* R. LADY WINDERMERE *is at table* R., *arranging roses in a blue bowl.*

(*Enter* PARKER.)

PARKER. Is your ladyship at home this afternoon?

LADY WINDERMERE. Yes—who has called?

PARKER. Lord Darlington, my lady.

LADY WINDERMERE (*hesitates for a moment*). Show him up—and I'm at home to anyone who calls.

PARKER. Yes, my lady. (*Exit* C.)

LADY WINDERMERE. It's best for me to see him before tonight. I'm glad he's come.

(*Enter* PARKER C.)

PARKER. Lord Darlington.

(*Enter* LORD DARLINGTON. *Exit* PARKER.)

39

LORD DARLINGTON. How do you do, Lady Windermere?

LADY WINDERMERE. How do you do, Lord Darlington? No, I can't shake hands with you. My hands are all wet with these roses. Aren't they lovely? They came up from Selby this morning.

LORD DARLINGTON. They are quite perfect. (*Sees a fan lying on the table.*) And what a wonderful fan! May I look at it?

LADY WINDERMERE. Do. Pretty, isn't it? It's got my name on it, and everything. I have only just seen it myself. It's my husband's birthday present to me. You know to-day is my birthday.

LORD DARLINGTON. No. Is it really?

LADY WINDERMERE. Yes; I'm of age to-day. Quite an important day in my life, isn't it? That is why I am giving this party to-night. Do sit down. (*Still arranging flowers.*)

LORD DARLINGTON (*sitting down*). I wish I had known it was your birthday, Lady Windermere. I would have covered the whole street in front of your house with flowers for you to walk on. They are made for you. (*A short pause.*)

LADY WINDERMERE. Lord Darlington, you annoyed me last night at the Foreign Office. I am afraid you are going to annoy me again.

LORD DARLINGTON. I, Lady Windermere?

(*Enter* PARKER *and* FOOTMAN C. *with tray and tea-things.*)

LADY WINDERMERE. Put it there, Parker. That will do. (*Wipes her hands with her pocket-handkerchief, goes to tea-table* L., *and sits down.*) Won't you come over, Lord Darlington? (*Exit* PARKER C.)

LORD DARLINGTON (*takes chair and goes across* L. C.). I am quite miserable, Lady Windermere. You must tell me what I did. (*Sits down at table* L.)

LADY WINDERMERE. Well, you kept paying me elaborate compliments the whole evening.

LORD DARLINGTON (*smiling*). Ah, now-a-days we are all of us so hard up, that the only pleasant things to pay *are* compliments. They're the only things we *can* pay.

LADY WINDERMERE (*shaking her head*). No, I am talking very seriously. You mustn't laugh, I am quite serious. I don't like compliments, and I don't see why a man should think he is pleasing a woman enormously when he says to her a whole heap of things that he doesn't mean.

LORD DARLINGTON. Ah, but I did mean them. (*Takes tea which she offers him.*)

LADY WINDERMERE (*gravely*). I hope not. I should be sorry to have to quarrel with you, Lord Darlington. I like you very much, you know that. But I shouldn't like you at all if I thought you were what most other men are. Believe me, you are better than most other men, and I sometimes think you pretend to be worse.

LORD DARLINGTON. We all have our little vanities, Lady Windermere.

LADY WINDERMERE. Why do you make that your special one? (*Still seated at table* L.)

LORD DARLINGTON (*still seated* L. C.). Oh, now-a-days so many conceited people go about society pretending to be good, that I think it shows rather a sweet and modest disposition to pretend to be bad. Besides, there is this to be said. If you pretend to be good, the world takes you very seriously. If you pretend to be bad, it doesn't. Such is the astounding stupidity of optimism.

LADY WINDERMERE. Don't you *want* the world to take you seriously, then, Lord Darlington?

LORD DARLINGTON. No, not the world. Who are the people the world takes seriously? All the dull people one can think of, from the Bishops down to the bores. I should like *you* to take me very seriously, Lady Windermere, *you* more than any one else in life.

LADY WINDERMERE. Why—why me?

LORD DARLINGTON (*after a slight hesitation*). Because

I think we might be great friends. Let us be great friends. You may want a friend some day.

LADY WINDERMERE. Why do you say that?

LORD DARLINGTON. Oh, we all want friends at times.

LADY WINDERMERE. I think we're very good friends already, Lord Darlington. We can always remain so as long as you don't——

LORD DARLINGTON. Don't what?

LADY WINDERMERE. Don't spoil it by saying extravagant silly things to me. You think I am a Puritan, I suppose? Well, I have something of the Puritan in me. I was brought up like that. I am glad of it. My mother died when I was a mere child. I lived always with Lady Julia, my father's eldest sister, you know. She was stern to me, but she taught me, what the world is forgetting, the difference that there is between what is right and what is wrong. *She* allowed of no compromise. *I* allow of none.

LORD DARLINGTON. My dear Lady Windermere!

LADY WINDERMERE (*leaning back on the sofa*). You look on me as being behind the age.—Well, I am! I should be sorry to be on the same level as an age like this.

LORD DARLINGTON. You think the age very bad?

LADY WINDERMERE. Yes. Now-a-days people seem to look on life as a speculation. It is not a speculation. It is a sacrament. Its ideal is Love. Its purification is sacrifice.

LORD DARLINGTON (*smiling*). Oh, anything is better than being sacrificed!

LADY WINDERMERE (*leaning forward*). Don't say that.

LORD DARLINGTON. I do say it. I feel it—I know it.

(*Enter* PARKER C.)

PARKER. The men want to know if they are to put the carpets on the terrace for to-night, my lady?

LADY WINDERMERE. You don't think it will rain, Lord Darlington, do you?

LORD DARLINGTON. I won't hear of it raining on your birthday!

LADY WINDERMERE. Tell them to do it at once, Parker.

(*Exit* PARKER C.)

LORD DARLINGTON (*still seated*). Do you think, then—of course I am only putting an imaginary instance—do you think that, in the case of a young married couple, say about two years married, if the husband suddenly becomes the intimate friend of a woman of—well, more than doubtful character, is always calling upon her, lunching with her, and probably paying her bills—do you think that the wife should not console herself?

LADY WINDERMERE (*frowning*). Console herself?

LORD DARLINGTON. Yes, I think she should—I think she has the right.

LADY WINDERMERE. Because the husband is vile—should the wife be vile also?

LORD DARLINGTON. Vileness is a terrible word, Lady Windermere.

LADY WINDERMERE. It is a terrible thing, Lord Darlington.

LORD DARLINGTON. Do you know, I am afraid that good people do a great deal of harm in this world. Certainly the greatest harm they do is that they make badness of such extraordinary importance. It is absurd to divide people into good and bad. People are either charming or tedious. I take the side of the charming, and you, Lady Windermere, can't help belonging to them.

LADY WINDERMERE. Now, Lord Darlington. (*Rising and crossing* R., *front of him.*) Don't stir, I am merely going to finish my flowers. (*Goes to table* R. C.)

LORD DARLINGTON (*rising and moving chair*). And I must say I think you are very hard on modern life, Lady

Windermere. Of course there is much against it, I admit. Most women, for instance, now-a-days, are rather mercenary.

LADY WINDERMERE. Don't talk about such people.

LORD DARLINGTON. Well, then, setting mercenary people aside, who, of course, are dreadful, do you think seriously that women who have committed what the world calls a fault should never be forgiven?

LADY WINDERMERE (*standing at table*). I think they should never be forgiven.

LORD DARLINGTON. And men? Do you think that there should be the same laws for men as there are for women?

LADY WINDERMERE. Certainly!

LORD DARLINGTON. I think life too complex a thing to be settled by these hard and fast rules.

LADY WINDERMERE. If we had "these hard and fast rules," we should find life much more simple.

LORD DARLINGTON. You allow of no exceptions?

LADY WINDERMERE. None!

LORD DARLINGTON. Ah, what a fascinating Puritan you are, Lady Windermere!

LADY WINDERMERE. The adjective was unnecessary, Lord Darlington.

LORD DARLINGTON. I couldn't help it. I can resist everything except temptation.

LADY WINDERMERE. You have the modern affectation of weakness.

LORD DARLINGTON (*looking at her*). It's only an affectation, Lady Windermere.

(*Enter* PARKER C.)

PARKER. The Duchess of Berwick and Lady Agatha Carlisle.

(*Enter the* DUCHESS OF BERWICK *and* LADY AGATHA CARLISLE C. *Exit* PARKER C.)

DUCHESS OF BERWICK (*coming down* c. *and shaking hands*). Dear Margaret, I am so pleased to see you. You remember Agatha, don't you? (*Crossing* L. C.) How do you do, Lord Darlington? I won't let you know my daughter, you are far too wicked.

LORD DARLINGTON. Don't say that, Duchess. As a wicked man I am a complete failure. Why, there are lots of people who say I have never really done anything wrong in the whole course of my life. Of course they only say it behind my back.

DUCHESS OF BERWICK. Isn't he dreadful? Agatha, this is Lord Darlington. Mind you don't believe a word he says. (LORD DARLINGTON *crosses* R. C.) No, no tea, thank you, dear. (*Crosses and sits on sofa.*) We have just had tea at Lady Markby's. Such bad tea, too. It was quite undrinkable. I wasn't at all surprised. Her own son-in-law supplies it. Agatha is looking forward so much to your ball to-night, dear Margaret.

LADY WINDERMERE (*seated* L. C.). Oh, you mustn't think it is going to be a ball, Duchess. It is only a dance in honor of my birthday. A small and early.

LORD DARLINGTON (*standing* L. C.). Very small, very early, and very select, Duchess.

DUCHESS OF BERWICK (*on sofa* L.). Of course it's going to be select. But we know *that*, dear Margaret, about *your* house. It is really one of the few houses in London where I can take Agatha, and where I feel perfectly secure about poor Berwick. I don't know what society is coming to. The most dreadful people seem to go everywhere. They certainly come to my parties—the men get quite furious if one doesn't ask them. Really, some one should make a stand against it.

LADY WINDERMERE. *I* will, Duchess. I will have no one in my house about whom there is any scandal.

LORD DARLINGTON (R. C.). Oh, don't say that, Lady Windermere. I should never be admitted! (*Sitting.*)

DUCHESS OF BERWICK. Oh, men don't matter. With

women it is different. We're good. Some of us are, at least. But we are positively getting elbowed into the corner. Our husbands would really forget our existence if we didn't nag at them from time to time, just to remind them that we have a perfect legal right to do so.

LORD DARLINGTON. It's a curious thing, Duchess, about the game of marriage—a game, by the way, that is going out of fashion—the wives hold all the honors and invariably lose the odd trick.

DUCHESS OF BERWICK. The odd trick? Is that the husband, Lord Darlington?

LORD DARLINGTON. It would be rather a good name for the modern husband.

DUCHESS OF BERWICK. Dear Lord Darlington, how thoroughly depraved you are!

LADY WINDERMERE. Lord Darlington is trivial.

LORD DARLINGTON. Ah, don't say that, Lady Windermere.

LADY WINDERMERE. Why do you *talk* so trivially about life, then?

LORD DARLINGTON. Because I think that life is far too important a thing ever to talk seriously about it. (*Moves* UP C.)

DUCHESS OF BERWICK. What does he mean? Do, as a concession to my poor wits, Lord Darlington, just explain to me what you really mean?

LORD DARLINGTON (*coming* DOWN *back of table*). I think I had better not, Duchess. Now-a-days to be intelligible is to be found out. Good-bye! (*Shakes hands with* DUCHESS.) And now (*goes* UP *stage*), Lady Windermere, good-bye. I may come to-night, mayn't I? Do let me come.

LADY WINDERMERE (*standing up stage with* LORD DARLINGTON). Yes, certainly. But you are not to say foolish, insincere things to people.

LORD DARLINGTON (*smiling*). Ah! you are beginning to reform me. It is a dangerous thing to reform any one, Lady Windermere. (*Bows, and exit* C.)

DUCHESS OF BERWICK (*who has risen, goes* C.). What a

charming, wicked creature! I like him so much. I'm quite
delighted he's gone! How sweet you're looking! Where
do you get your gowns? And now I must tell you how
sorry I am for you, dear Margaret. (*Crosses to sofa and
sits with* LADY WINDERMERE.) Agatha, darling!

LADY AGATHA. Yes, Mamma. (*Rises.*)

DUCHESS OF BERWICK. Will you go and look over the
photograph album that I see there?

LADY AGATHA. Yes, Mamma. (*Goes to table* L.)

DUCHESS OF BERWICK. Dear girl! She is so fond of
photographs of Switzerland. Such a pure taste, I think.
But I really am so sorry for you, Margaret.

LADY WINDERMERE (*smiling*). Why, Duchess?

DUCHESS OF BERWICK. Oh, on account of that horrid
woman. She dresses so well, too, which makes it much
worse, sets such a dreadful example. Augustus—you
know my disreputable brother—such a trial to us all—
well, Augustus is completely infatuated about her. It is
quite scandalous, for she is absolutely inadmissible into
society. Many a woman has a past, but I am told that she
has at least a dozen, and that they all fit.

LADY WINDERMERE. Whom are you talking about,
Duchess?

DUCHESS OF BERWICK. About Mrs. Erlynne.

LADY WINDERMERE. Mrs. Erlynne? I never heard of
her, Duchess. And what *has* she to do with me?

DUCHESS OF BERWICK. My poor child! Agatha, darling!

LADY AGATHA. Yes, Mamma.

DUCHESS OF BERWICK. Will you go out on the terrace
and look at the sunset?

LADY AGATHA. Yes, Mamma.

(*Exit through window* L.)

DUCHESS OF BERWICK. Sweet girl! So devoted to sun-
sets! Shows such refinement of feeling, does it not? After all, there is nothing like nature, is there?

LADY WINDERMERE. But what is it, Duchess? Why do you talk to me about this person?

DUCHESS OF BERWICK. Don't you really know? I assure you we're all so distressed about it. Only last night at dear Lady Fansen's every one was saying how extraordinary it was that, of all men in London, Windermere should behave in such a way.

LADY WINDERMERE. My husband—what has *he* got to do with any woman of that kind?

DUCHESS OF BERWICK. Ah, what indeed, dear? That is the point. He goes to see her continually, and stops for hours at a time, and while he is there she is not at home to any one. Not that many ladies call on her, dear, but she has a great many disreputable men friends—my own brother in particular, as I told you—and that is what makes it so dreadful about Windermere. We looked upon *him* as being such a model husband, but I am afraid there is no doubt about it. My dear nieces—you know the Saville girls, don't you?—such nice domestic creatures—plain, dreadfully plain, but so good—well, they're always at the window doing fancy work, and making ugly things for the poor, which I think so useful of them in these dreadful socialistic days, and this terrible woman has taken a house in Curzon Street, right opposite them—such a respectable street, too. I don't know what we're coming to! And they tell me that Windermere goes there four and five times a week—they *see* him. They can't help it—and although they never talk scandal, they—well, of course—they remark on it to every one. And the worst of it all is, that I have been told that this woman has got a great deal of money out of somebody, for it seems that she came to London six months ago without anything at all to speak of, and now she has this charming house in Mayfair, drives her pony in the Park every afternoon, and all—well, all—since she has known poor dear Windermere.

LADY WINDERMERE. Oh, I can't believe it!

DUCHESS OF BERWICK. But it's quite true, my dear. The whole of London knows it. That is why I felt it was better to come and talk to you, and advise you to take Windermere away at once to Homburg or to Aix, where he'll have something to amuse him, and where you can watch him all day long. I assure you, my dear, that on several occasions after I was first married I had to pretend to be very ill, and was obliged to drink the most unpleasant mineral waters, merely to get Berwick out of town. He was so extremely susceptible. Though I am bound to say he never gave away any large sums of money to anybody. He is far too high-principled for that.

LADY WINDERMERE (*interrupting*). Duchess, Duchess, it's impossible! (*Rising and crossing stage* C.) We are only married two years. Our child is but six months old. (*Sits in chair* R. *of* L. *table.*)

DUCHESS OF BERWICK. Ah, the dear pretty baby! How is the little darling? Is it a boy or a girl? I hope a girl—ah, no, I remember it's a boy! I'm so sorry. Boys are so wicked. My boy is excessively immoral. You wouldn't believe at what hours he comes home. And he's only left Oxford a few months—I really don't know what they teach them there.

LADY WINDERMERE. Are *all* men bad?

DUCHESS OF BERWICK. Oh, all of them, my dear, all of them, without any exception. And they never grow any better. Men become old, but they never become good.

LADY WINDERMERE. Windermere and I married for love.

DUCHESS OF BERWICK. Yes, we begin like that. It was only Berwick's brutal and incessant threats of suicide that made me accept him at all, and before the year was out he was running after all kinds of petticoats, every color, every shape, every material. In fact, before the honeymoon was over, I caught him winking at my maid, a most pretty, respectable girl. I dismissed her at once without a character.—No, I remember I passed her on

to my sister; poor dear Sir George is so shortsighted, I
thought it wouldn't matter. But it did, though it was most
unfortunate. (*Rises.*) And now, my dear child, I must go,
as we are dining out. And mind you don't take this little
aberration of Windermere's too much to heart. Just take
him abroad, and he'll come back to you all right.

LADY WINDERMERE. Come back to me? (C.)

DUCHESS OF BERWICK (L. C.). Yes, dear, these wicked
women get our husbands away from us, but they always
come back, slightly damaged, of course. And don't make
scenes, men hate them!

LADY WINDERMERE. It is very kind of you, Duchess, to
come and tell me this. But I can't believe that my husband is untrue to me.

DUCHESS OF BERWICK. Pretty child! I was like that
once. Now I know that all men are monsters. (LADY
WINDERMERE *rings bell.*) The only thing to do is to feed
the wretches well. A good cook does wonders, and that
I know you have. My dear Margaret, you are not going
to cry?

LADY WINDERMERE. You needn't be afraid, Duchess,
I never cry.

DUCHESS OF BERWICK. That's quite right, dear. Crying
is the refuge of plain women, but the ruin of pretty ones.
Agatha, darling!

LADY AGATHA (*entering* L.). Yes, Mamma. (*Stands
back of table* L. C.)

DUCHESS OF BERWICK. Come and bid good-bye to
Lady Windermere, and thank her for your charming
visit. (*Coming down again.*) And by the way, I must
thank you for sending a card to Mr. Hopper—he's that
rich young Australian people are taking such notice of
just at present. His father made a great fortune by sell-
ing some kind of food in circular tins—most palatable,
I believe—I fancy it is the thing the servants always
refuse to eat. But the son is quite interesting. I think
he's attracted by dear Agatha's clever talk. Of course,

we should be very sorry to lose her, but I think that a mother who doesn't part with a daughter every season has no real affection. We're coming to-night, dear. (PARKER *opens* C. *doors.*) And remember my advice, take the poor fellow out of town at once, it is the only thing to do. Good-bye, once more; come, Agatha.

(*Exeunt* DUCHESS *and* LADY AGATHA C.)

LADY WINDERMERE. How horrible! I understand now what Lord Darlington meant by the imaginary instance of the couple not two years married. Oh, it can't be true—she spoke of enormous sums of money paid to this woman. I know where Arthur keeps his bank book—in one of the drawers of that desk. I might find out by that. I *will* find out. (*Opens drawer.*) No, it is some hideous mistake. (*Rises and goes* C.) Some silly scandal! He loves *me*! He loves *me*! But why should I not look? I am his wife, I have a right to look! (*Returns to bureau, takes out book and examines it, page by page, smiles and gives a sigh of relief.*) I knew it, there is not a word of truth in this stupid story. (*Puts book back in drawer. As she does so, starts and takes out another book.*) A second book—private—locked! (*Tries to open it, but fails. Sees paper knife on bureau, and with it cuts cover from book. Begins to start at the first page.*) Mrs. Erlynne—£600—Mrs. Erlynne—£700—Mrs. Erylnne—£400. Oh! it is true! it is true! How horrible! (*Throws book on floor.*)

(*Enter* LORD WINDERMERE C.)

LORD WINDERMERE. Well, dear, has the fan been sent home yet? (*Going* R. C. *sees book.*) Margaret, you have cut open my bank book. You have no right to do such a thing!

LADY WINDERMERE. You think it wrong that you are found out, don't you?

LORD WINDERMERE. I think it wrong that a wife should spy on her husband.

LADY WINDERMERE. I did not spy on you. I never knew of this woman's existence till half an hour ago. Some one who pitied me was kind enough to tell me what every one in London knows already—your daily visits to Curzon Street, your mad infatuation, the monstrous sums of money you squander on this infamous woman! (*Crossing* L.)

LORD WINDERMERE. Margaret, don't talk like that of Mrs. Erlynne, you don't know how unjust it is!

LADY WINDERMERE (*turning to him*). You are very jealous of Mrs. Erlynne's honor. I wish you had been as jealous of mine.

LORD WINDERMERE. Your honor is untouched, Margaret. You don't think for a moment that—— (*Puts book back into desk.*)

LADY WINDERMERE. I think that you spend your money strangely. That is all. Oh, don't imagine I mind about the money. As far as I am concerned, you may squander everything we have. But what I *do* mind is that you who have loved me, you who have taught me to love you, should pass from the love that is given to the love that is bought. Oh, it's horrible! (*Sits on sofa.*) And it is I who feel degraded. You don't feel anything. I feel stained, utterly stained. You can't realize how hideous the last six months seem to me now—every kiss you have given me is tainted in my memory.

LORD WINDERMERE (*crossing to her*). Don't say that, Margaret. I never loved any one in the whole world but you.

LADY WINDERMERE (*rises*). Who is this woman, then? Why do you take a house for her?

LORD WINDERMERE. I did not take a house for her.

LADY WINDERMERE. You gave her the money to do it, which is the same thing.

LORD WINDERMERE. Margaret, as far as I have known Mrs. Erlynne——

LADY WINDERMERE. Is there a Mr. Erlynne—or is he a myth?

LORD WINDERMERE. Her husband died many years ago. She is alone in the world.

LADY WINDERMERE. No relations? (*A pause.*)

LORD WINDERMERE. None.

LADY WINDERMERE. Rather curious, isn't it? (L.)

LORD WINDERMERE (L. C.). Margaret, I was saying to you—and I beg you to listen to me—that as far as I have known Mrs. Erlynne, she has conducted herself well. If years ago——

LADY WINDERMERE. Oh! (*Crossing* R. C.) I don't want details about her life.

LORD WINDERMERE. I am not going to give you any details about her life. I tell you simply this—Mrs. Erlynne was once honored, loved, respected. She was well born, she had a position—she lost everything—threw it away, if you like. That makes it all the more bitter. Misfortunes one can endure—they come from outside, they are accidents. But to suffer for one's own faults—ah! there is the sting of life. It was twenty years ago, too. She was little more than a girl then. She had been a wife for even less time than you have.

LADY WINDERMERE. I am not interested in her—and—you should not mention this woman and me in the same breath. It is an error of taste. (*Sitting* R. *at desk.*)

LORD WINDERMERE. Margaret, you could save this woman. She wants to get back into society, and she wants you to help her. (*Crossing to her.*)

LADY WINDERMERE. Me!

LORD WINDERMERE. Yes, you.

LADY WINDERMERE. How impertinent of her! (*A pause.*)

LORD WINDERMERE. Margaret, I came to ask you a great favour, and I still ask it of you, though you have discovered what I had intended you should never have known, that I have given Mrs. Erlynne a large sum of money. I want you to send her an invitation for our party to-night. (*Standing* L. *of her.*)

LADY WINDERMERE. You are mad. (*Rises.*)

LORD WINDERMERE. I entreat you. People may chatter about her, do chatter about her, of course, but they don't know anything definite about her. She has been to several houses—not to houses where you would go, I admit, but still to houses where women who are in what is called Society now-a-days do go. That does not content her. She wants you to receive her once.

LADY WINDERMERE. As a triumph for her, I suppose?

LORD WINDERMERE. No; but because she knows that you are a good woman—and that if she comes here once she will have a chance of a happier, a surer life than she has had. She will make no further effort to know you. Won't you help a woman who is trying to get back?

LADY WINDERMERE. No! If a woman really repents, she never wishes to return to the society that has made or seen her ruin.

LORD WINDERMERE. I beg of you.

LADY WINDERMERE (*crossing to door* R.). I am going to dress for dinner, and don't mention the subject again this evening. Arthur (*going to him* C.), you fancy because I have no father or mother that I am alone in the world and that you can treat me as you choose. You are wrong, I have friends, many friends.

LORD WINDERMERE (L. C.). Margaret, you are talking foolishly, recklessly. I won't argue with you, but I insist upon your asking Mrs. Erlynne to-night.

LADY WINDERMERE (R. C.). I shall do nothing of the kind. (*Crossing* L. C.)

LORD WINDERMERE. You refuse? (C.)

LADY WINDERMERE. Absolutely!

LORD WINDERMERE. Ah, Margaret, do this for my sake; it is her last chance.

LADY WINDERMERE. What has that to do with me?

LORD WINDERMERE. How hard good women are!

LADY WINDERMERE. How weak bad men are!

LORD WINDERMERE. Margaret, none of us men may be good enough for the women we marry—that is quite true—but you don't imagine I would ever—oh, the suggestion is monstrous!

LADY WINDERMERE. Why should *you* be different from other men? I am told that there is hardly a husband in London who does not waste his life over *some* shameful passion.

LORD WINDERMERE. I am not one of them.

LADY WINDERMERE. I am not sure of that!

LORD WINDERMERE. You are sure in your heart. But don't make chasm after chasm between us. God knows the last few minutes have thrust us wide enough apart. Sit down and write the card.

LADY WINDERMERE. Nothing in the whole world would induce me.

LORD WINDERMERE (*crossing to the bureau*). Then I will. (*Rings electric bell, sits, and writes card.*)

LADY WINDERMERE. You are going to invite this woman? (*Crossing to him.*)

LORD WINDERMERE. Yes. (*Pause.*)

(*Enter* PARKER.)

LORD WINDERMERE. Parker!

PARKER. Yes, my lord. (*Comes* DOWN L. C.)

LORD WINDERMERE. Have this note sent to Mrs. Erlynne at No. 84A Curzon Street. (*Crossing to* L. C. *and giving note to* PARKER.) There is no answer. (*Exit* PARKER C.)

LADY WINDERMERE. Arthur, if that woman comes here, I shall insult her.

LORD WINDERMERE. Margaret, don't say that.

LADY WINDERMERE. I mean it.

LORD WINDERMERE. Child, if you did such a thing, there's not a woman in London who wouldn't pity you.

LADY WINDERMERE. There is not a *good* woman in London who would not applaud me. We have been too lax. We must make an example. I propose to begin to-night. (*Picking up fan.*) Yes, you gave me this fan to-day; it was your birthday present. If that woman crosses my threshold, I shall strike her across the face with it.

LORD WINDERMERE. Margaret, you couldn't do such a thing.

LADY WINDERMERE. You don't know me! (*Moves* R.)

(*Enter* PARKER.)

LADY WINDERMERE. Parker!

PARKER. Yes, my lady.

LADY WINDERMERE. I shall dine in my own room. I don't want dinner, in fact. See that everything is ready by half-past ten. And, Parker, be sure you pronounce the names of the guests very distinctly to-night. Sometimes you speak so fast that I miss them. I am particularly anxious to hear the names quite clearly, so as to make no mistake. You understand, Parker?

PARKER. Yes, my lady.

LADY WINDERMERE. That will do! (*Exit* PARKER C. *Speaking to* LORD WINDERMERE.) Arthur, if that woman comes here—I warn you——

LORD WINDERMERE. Margaret, you'll ruin us!

LADY WINDERMERE. Us! From this moment my life is separate from yours. But if you wish to avoid a public scandal, write at once to this woman, and tell her that I forbid her to come here!

LORD WINDERMERE. I will not—I cannot—she must come!

LADY WINDERMERE. Then I shall do exactly as I have said. (*Goes* R.) You leave me no choice. (*Exit* R.)

LORD WINDERMERE (*calling after her*). Margaret! Margaret! (*A pause.*) My God! What shall I do! I dare not tell her who this woman really is. The shame would kill her. (*Sinks down into a chair and buries his face in his hands.*)

CURTAIN

ACT II

SCENE.—*Drawing-room in* LORD WINDERMERE'S *house. Door* R. U. *opening into ballroom, where band is playing. Door* L. *through which guests are entering. Door* L. U. *opens on an illuminated terrace. Palms, flowers, and brilliant lights. Room crowded with guests.* LADY WINDERMERE *is receiving them.*

DUCHESS OF BERWICK (UP C.). So strange Lord Windermere isn't here. Mr. Hopper is very late, too. You have kept those five dances for him, Agatha! (*Comes* DOWN.)

LADY AGATHA. Yes, Mamma.

DUCHESS OF BERWICK (*sitting on sofa*). Just let me see your card. I'm so glad Lady Windermere has revived cards.—They're a mother's only safeguard. You dear simple little thing! (*Scratches out two names.*) No nice girl should ever waltz with such particularly younger sons! It looks so fast! The last two dances you must pass on the terrace with Mr. Hopper.

(*Enter* MR. DUMBY *and* LADY PLYMDALE *from the ballroom.*)

LADY AGATHA. Yes, Mamma.

DUCHESS OF BERWICK (*fanning herself*). The air is so pleasant here.

PARKER. Mrs. Cowper-Cowper. Lady Stutfield. Sir James Royston. Mr. Guy Berkeley. (*These people enter as announced.*)

DUMBY. Good-evening, Lady Stutfield. I suppose this will be the last ball of the season.

LADY STUTFIELD. I suppose so, Mr. Dumby. It's been a delightful season, hasn't it?

DUMBY. Quite delightful! Good-evening, Duchess. I suppose this will be the last ball of the season?

DUCHESS OF BERWICK. I suppose so, Mr. Dumby. It has been a very dull season, hasn't it?

DUMBY. Dreadfully dull! Dreadfully dull!

MRS. COWPER-COWPER. Good-evening, Mr. Dumby. I suppose this will be the last ball of the season?

DUMBY. Oh, I think not. There'll probably be two more. (*Wanders back to* LADY PLYMDALE.)

PARKER. Mr. Rufford. Lady Jedburgh and Miss Graham. Mr. Hopper. (*These people enter as announced.*)

HOPPER. How do you do, Lady Windermere? How do you do, Duchess? (*Bows to* LADY AGATHA.)

DUCHESS OF BERWICK. Dear Mr. Hopper, how nice of you to come so early. We all know how you are run after in London.

HOPPER. Capital place, London! They are not nearly so exclusive in London as they are in Sydney.

DUCHESS OF BERWICK. Ah! we know your value, Mr. Hopper. We wish there were more like you. It would make life so much easier. Do you know, Mr. Hopper, dear Agatha and I are so much interested in Australia. It must be so pretty with all the dear little kangaroos flying about. Agatha has found it on the map. What a curious shape it is! Just like a large packing-case. However, it is a very young country, isn't it?

HOPPER. Wasn't it made at the same time as the others, Duchess?

DUCHESS OF BERWICK. How clever you are, Mr. Hop-

per. You have a cleverness quite of your own. Now I
mustn't keep you.

HOPPER. But I should like to dance with Lady Agatha,
Duchess.

DUCHESS OF BERWICK. Well, I *hope* she has a dance
left. Have you got a dance left, Agatha?

LADY AGATHA. Yes, Mamma.

DUCHESS OF BERWICK. The next one?

LADY AGATHA. Yes, Mamma.

HOPPER. May I have the pleasure? (LADY AGATHA
bows.)

DUCHESS OF BERWICK. Mind you take great care of
my little chatterbox, Mr. Hopper. (LADY AGATHA *and*
MR. HOPPER *pass into ballroom.*)

(*Enter* LORD WINDERMERE L.)

LORD WINDERMERE. Margaret, I want to speak to you.

LADY WINDERMERE. In a moment. (*The music stops.*)

PARKER. Lord Augustus Lorton.

(*Enter* LORD AUGUSTUS LORTON.)

LORD AUGUSTUS. Good-evening, Lady Windermere.

DUCHESS OF BERWICK. Sir James, will you take me
into the ballroom? Augustus has been dining with us to-
night. I really have had quite enough of dear Augustus
for the moment. (SIR JAMES R. *gives the* DUCHESS *his arm
and escorts her into the ballroom.*)

PARKER. Mr. and Mrs. Arthur Bowden. Lord and
Lady Paisley. Lord Darlington. (*These people enter as
announced.*)

LORD AUGUSTUS (*coming up to* LORD WINDERMERE).
Want to speak to you particularly, dear boy. I'm worn
to a shadow. Know I don't look it. None of us men
do look what we really are. Demmed good thing, too.

What I want to know is this. Who is she? Where does she come from? Why hasn't she got any demmed relations? Demmed nuisance, relations! But they make one so demmed respectable.

LORD WINDERMERE. You are talking of Mrs. Erlynne, I suppose. I only met her six months ago. Till then I never knew of her existence.

LORD AUGUSTUS. You have seen a good deal of her since then.

LORD WINDERMERE (*coldly*). Yes, I have seen a good deal of her since then. I have just seen her.

LORD AUGUSTUS. Egad! the women are very down on her. I have been dining with Arabella this evening. By Jove! you should have heard what she said about Mrs. Erlynne. She didn't leave a rag on her.... (*Aside.*) Berwick and I told her that didn't matter much, as the lady in question must have an extremely fine figure. You should have seen Arabella's expression! ... But, look here, dear boy. I don't know what to do about Mrs. Erlynne. Egad! I might be married to her, she treats me with such demmed indifference. She's deuced clever, too! She explains everything. Egad! She explains you. She has got any amount of explanations for you—and all of them different.

LORD WINDERMERE. No explanations are necessary about my friendship with Mrs. Erlynne.

LORD AUGUSTUS. Hem! Well, look here, dear old fellow. Do you think she will ever get into this demmed thing called Society? Would you introduce her to your wife? No use beating about the confounded bush. Would you do that?

LORD WINDERMERE. Mrs. Erlynne is coming here tonight.

LORD AUGUSTUS. Your wife has sent her a card?

LORD WINDERMERE. Mrs. Erlynne has received a card.

LORD AUGUSTUS. Then she's all right, dear boy. But why didn't you tell me that before? It would have saved me a heap of worry and demmed misunderstandings!

(LADY AGATHA *and* MR. HOPPER *cross and exit on terrace* L. U. E.)

PARKER. Mr. Cecil Graham! (*Enter* MR. CECIL GRAHAM.)

CECIL GRAHAM (*bows to* LADY WINDERMERE, *passes over and shakes hands with* LORD WINDERMERE). Good evening, Arthur. Why don't you ask me how I am? I like people to ask me how I am. It shows a widespread interest in my health. Now to-night I am not at all well. Been dining with my people. Wonder why it is one's people are always so tedious? My father would talk morality after dinner. I told him he was old enough to know better. But my experience is that as soon as people are old enough to know better, they don't know anything at all. Hullo, Tuppy! Hear you're going to be married again; thought you were tired of that game.

LORD AUGUSTUS. You're excessively trivial, my dear boy, excessively trivial!

CECIL GRAHAM. By the way, Tuppy, which is it? Have you been twice married and once divorced, or twice divorced and once married? I say, you've been twice divorced and once married. It seems so much more probable.

LORD AUGUSTUS. I have a very bad memory. I really don't remember which. (*Moves away* R.)

LADY PLYMDALE. Lord Windermere, I've something most particular to ask you.

LORD WINDERMERE. I am afraid—if you will excuse me—I must join my wife.

LADY PLYMDALE. Oh, you mustn't dream of such a thing. It's most dangerous now-a-days for a husband to pay any attention to his wife in public. It always makes people think that he beats her when they're alone. The world has grown so suspicious of anything that looks like a happy married life. But I'll tell you what it is at supper. (*Moves towards door of ballroom.*)

LORD WINDERMERE (C.). Margaret, I *must* speak to you.

LADY WINDERMERE. Will you hold my fan for me, Lord Darlington? Thanks. (*Comes* DOWN *to him.*)

LORD WINDERMERE (*crossing to her*). Margaret, what you said before dinner was, of course, impossible?

LADY WINDERMERE. That woman is not coming here to-night!

LORD WINDERMERE (R. C.). Mrs. Erlynne is coming here, and if you in any way annoy or wound her, you will bring shame and sorrow on us both. Remember that! Ah, Margaret! only trust me! A wife should trust her husband!

LADY WINDERMERE (C.). London is full of women who trust their husbands. One can always recognize them. They look so thoroughly unhappy. I am not going to be one of them. (*Moves* UP.) Lord Darlington, will you give me back my fan, please? Thanks . . . A useful thing, a fan, isn't it? . . . I want a friend to-night, Lord Darlington. I didn't know I would want one so soon.

LORD DARLINGTON. Lady Windermere! I knew the time would come some day; but why to-night?

LORD WINDERMERE. I *will* tell her. I must. It would be terrible if there were any scene. Margaret——

PARKER. Mrs. Erlynne. (MRS. ERLYNNE *enters, very beautifully dressed and very dignified.* LADY WINDERMERE *clutches at her fan, then lets it drop on the floor. She bows coldly to* MRS. ERLYNNE, *who bows to her sweetly in turn, and sails into the room.*)

LORD DARLINGTON. You have dropped your fan, Lady Windermere. (*Picks it up and hands it to her.*)

MRS. ERLYNNE (C.). How do you do, again, Lord Windermere? How charming your sweet wife looks! Quite a picture!

LORD WINDERMERE (*in a low voice*). It was terribly rash of you to come!

MRS. ERLYNNE (*smiling*). The wisest thing I ever did

in my life. And, by the way, you must pay me a good deal of attention this evening. I am afraid of the women. You must introduce me to some of them. The men I can always manage. How do you do, Lord Augustus? You have quite neglected me lately. I have not seen you since yesterday. I am afraid you're faithless. Everyone told me so.

LORD AUGUSTUS (R.). Now really, Mrs. Erlynne, allow me to explain.

MRS. ERLYNNE (R. C.). No, dear Lord Augustus, you can't explain anything. It is your chief charm.

LORD AUGUSTUS. Ah! if you find charms in me, Mrs. Erlynne—— (*They converse together.* LORD WINDER-MERE *moves uneasily about the room, watching* MRS. ERLYNNE.)

LORD DARLINGTON (*to* LADY WINDERMERE). How pale you are!

LADY WINDERMERE. Cowards are always pale.

LORD DARLINGTON. You look faint. Come out on the terrace.

LADY WINDERMERE. Yes. (*To* PARKER.) Parker, send my cloak out.

MRS. ERLYNNE (*crossing to her*). Lady Windermere, how beautifully your terrace is illuminated. Reminds me of Prince Doria's at Rome. (LADY WINDERMERE *bows coldly, and goes off with* LORD DARLINGTON.) Oh, how do you do, Mr. Graham? Isn't that your aunt, Lady Jedburgh? I should so much like to know her.

CECIL GRAHAM (*after a moment's hesitation and embarrassment*). Oh, certainly, if you wish it. Aunt Caroline, allow me to introduce Mrs. Erlynne.

MRS. ERLYNNE. So pleased to meet you, Lady Jedburgh. (*Sits beside her on the sofa.*) Your nephew and I are great friends. I am so much interested in his political career. I think he's sure to be a wonderful success. He thinks like a Tory, and talks like a Radical, and that's so important now-a-days. He's such a brilliant talker, too.

But we all know from whom he inherits that. Lord Allandale was saying to me only yesterday in the Park that Mr. Graham talks almost as well as his aunt.

LADY JEDBURGH (R.). Most kind of you to say these charming things to me! (MRS. ERLYNNE *smiles and continues conversation.*)

DUMBY (*to* CECIL GRAHAM). Did you introduce Mrs. Erlynne to Lady Jedburgh?

CECIL GRAHAM. Had to, my dear fellow. Couldn't help it. That woman can make one do anything she wants. How, I don't know.

DUMBY. Hope to goodness she won't speak to me! (*Saunters towards* LADY PLYMDALE.)

MRS. ERLYNNE (C. *to* LADY JEDBURGH). On Thursday? With great pleasure. (*Rises and speaks to* LORD WINDERMERE, *laughing.*) What a bore it is to have to be civil to these old dowagers. But they always insist on it.

LADY PLYMDALE (*to* MR. DUMBY). Who is that well-dressed woman talking to Windermere?

DUMBY. Haven't got the slightest idea. Looks like an *edition de luxe* of a wicked French novel, meant specially for the English market.

MRS. ERLYNNE. So that is poor Dumby with Lady Plymdale? I hear she is frightfully jealous of him. He doesn't seem anxious to speak to me to-night. I suppose he is afraid of her. Those straw-colored women have dreadful tempers. Do you know, I think I'll dance with you first, Windermere. (LORD WINDERMERE *bites his lip and frowns.*) It will make Lord Augustus so jealous! Lord Augustus! (LORD AUGUSTUS *comes down.*) Lord Windermere insists on my dancing with him first, and, as it's his own house, I can't well refuse. You know I would much sooner dance with you.

LORD AUGUSTUS (*with a low bow*). I wish I could think so, Mrs. Erlynne.

MRS. ERLYNNE. You know it far too well. I can fancy

a person dancing through life with you and finding it charming.

LORD AUGUSTUS (*placing his hand on his white waist-coat*). Oh, thank you, thank you, thank you. You are the most adorable of all ladies!

MRS. ERLYNNE. What a nice speech! So simple and so sincere! Just the sort of speech I like. Well, you shall hold my bouquet. (*Goes towards ballroom on* LORD WINDERMERE'*s arm.*) Ah, Mr. Dumby, how are you? I am so sorry I have been out the last three times you have called. Come and lunch on Friday.

DUMBY (*with perfect nonchalance*). Delighted. (LADY PLYMDALE *glares with indignation at* MR. DUMBY. LORD AUGUSTUS *follows* MRS. ERLYNNE *and* LORD WINDERMERE *into the ballroom, holding bouquet.*)

LADY PLYMDALE (*to* MR. DUMBY). What an absolute brute you are! I never can believe a word you say! Why did you tell me you didn't know her? What do you mean by calling on her three times running? You are not to go to lunch there; of course you understand that?

DUMBY. My dear Laura, I wouldn't dream of going!

LADY PLYMDALE. You haven't told me her name yet! Who is she?

DUMBY (*coughs slightly and smoothes his hair*). She's a Mrs. Erlynne.

LADY PLYMDALE. *That* woman!

DUMBY. Yes, that is what everyone calls her.

LADY PLYMDALE. How very interesting! How intensely interesting! I really must have a good stare at her. (*Goes to door of ballroom and looks in.*) I have heard the most shocking things about her. They say she is running poor Windermere. And Lady Windermere, who goes in for being so proper, invites her! How extremely amusing! It takes a thoroughly good woman to do a thoroughly stupid thing. You are to lunch there on Friday!

DUMBY. Why?

LADY PLYMDALE. Because I want you to take my husband with you. He has been so attentive lately that he has become a perfect nuisance. Now this woman is just the thing for him. He'll dance attendance upon her as long as she lets him, and won't bother me. I assure you, women of that kind are most useful. They form the basis of other people's marriages.

DUMBY. What a mystery you are!

LADY PLYMDALE (*looking at him*). I wish *you* were!

DUMBY. I am—to myself. I am the only person in the world I should like to know thoroughly; but I don't see any chance of it just at present. (*They pass into the ballroom, and* LADY WINDERMERE *and* LORD DARLINGTON *enter from the terrace.*)

LADY WINDERMERE. Yes. Her coming here is monstrous, unbearable. I know now what you meant to-day at teatime. Why didn't you tell me right out? You should have.

LORD DARLINGTON. I couldn't. A man can't tell these things about another man. But if I had known he was going to make you ask her here to-night, I think I would have told you. That insult, at any rate, you would have been spared.

LADY WINDERMERE. I did not ask her. He insisted on her coming—against my entreaties—against my commands. Oh! the house is tainted for me! I feel that every woman here sneers at me as she dances by with my husband. What have I done to deserve this? I gave him all my life. He took it—used it—spoiled it! I am degraded in my own eyes; and I lack courage—I am a coward! (*Sits down on sofa.*)

LORD DARLINGTON. If I know you at all, I know that you can't live with a man who treats you like this. What sort of life would you have with him? You would feel that he was lying to you every moment of the day. You would feel that the look in his eyes was false, his voice false, his touch false, his passion false. He would come to you when he was weary of others; you would have to comfort him. He would come to you when he was devoted to others; you would have to charm him. You would have to be to him the mask of his real life, the cloak to hide his secret.

LADY WINDERMERE. You are right—you are terribly right. But where am I to turn? You said you would be my friend, Lord Darlington.—Tell me, what am I to do? Be my friend now.

LORD DARLINGTON. Between men and women there is no friendship possible. There is passion, enmity, worship, love, but no friendship. I love you——

LADY WINDERMERE. No, no! (*Rises.*)

LORD DARLINGTON. Yes, I love you! You are more to me than anything in the whole world. What does your husband give you? Nothing. Whatever is in him he gives to this wretched woman, whom he has thrust into your society, into your home, to shame you before everyone. I offer you my life——

LADY WINDERMERE. Lord Darlington!

LORD DARLINGTON. My life—my whole life. Take it, and do with it what you will. . . . I love you—love you as I have never loved any living thing. From the moment I met you I loved you, loved you blindly, adoringly, madly! You did not know it then—you know it now! Leave this house to-night. I won't tell you that the world matters nothing, or the world's voice, or the voice of society. They matter a good deal. They matter far too much. But there are moments when one has to choose between living one's own life, fully, entirely, completely—or dragging out some false, shallow, degrading existence that the world in its hypocrisy demands. You have that moment now. Choose! Oh, my love, choose!

LADY WINDERMERE (*moving slowly away from him and looking at him with startled eyes*). I have not the courage.

LORD DARLINGTON (*following her*). Yes; you have the

courage. There may be six months of pain, of disgrace
even, but when you no longer bear his name, when you
bear mine, all will be well. Margaret, my love, my wife
that shall be some day—yes, my wife! You know it! What
are you now? This woman has the place that belongs by
right to you. Oh, go—go out of this house, with head
erect, with a smile upon your lips, with courage in your
eyes. All London will know why you did it; and who will
blame you? No one. If they do, what matter? Wrong?
What is wrong? It's wrong for a man to abandon his wife
for a shameless woman. It is wrong for a wife to remain
with a man who so dishonours her. You said once you
would make no compromise with things. Make none
now. Be brave! Be yourself!

LADY WINDERMERE. I am afraid of being myself. Let
me think! Let me wait! My husband may return to me.
(*Sits down on sofa.*)

LORD DARLINGTON. And you would take him back!
You are not what I thought you were. You are just the
same as every other woman. You would stand anything
rather than face the censure of a world whose praise you
would despise. In a week you will be driving with this
woman in the Park. She will be your constant guest—
your dearest friend. You would endure anything rather
than break with one blow this monstrous lie. You are
right. You have no courage; none!

LADY WINDERMERE. Ah, give me time to think. I cannot answer you now. (*Passes her hand nervously over her
brow.*)

LORD DARLINGTON. It must be now or not at all.

LADY WINDERMERE (*rising from the sofa*). Then not at
all! (*A pause.*)

LORD DARLINGTON. You break my heart!

LADY WINDERMERE. Mine is already broken. (*A pause.*)

LORD DARLINGTON. To-morrow I leave England. This
is the last time I shall ever look on you. You will never
see me again. For one moment our lives met—our souls

touched. They must never meet or touch again. Good-bye, Margaret.

(*Exit.*)

LADY WINDERMERE. How alone I am in life! How terribly alone! (*The music stops. Enter the* DUCHESS OF BERWICK *and* LORD PLYMDALE, *laughing and talking. Other guests come on from the ballroom.*)

DUCHESS OF BERWICK. Dear Margaret, I've just been having such a delightful chat with Mrs. Erlynne. I am so sorry for what I said to you this afternoon about her. Of course she must be all right if *you* invite her. A most attractive woman, and has such sensible views on life. Told me she entirely disapproved of people marrying more than once, so I feel quite safe about poor Augustus. Can't imagine why people speak against her. It's those horrid nieces of mine—the Saville girls—they're always talking scandal. Still, I should go to Homburg, dear, I really should. She is just a little too attractive. But where is Agatha? Oh, there she is. (LADY AGATHA *and* MR. HOPPER *enter from the terrace* L. U. E.) Mr. Hopper, I am very angry with you. You have taken Agatha out on the terrace, and she is so delicate.

HOPPER (L. C.). Awfully sorry, Duchess. We went out for a moment and then got chatting together.

DUCHESS OF BERWICK (C.). Ah, about dear Australia, I suppose?

HOPPER. Yes.

DUCHESS OF BERWICK. Agatha, darling! (*Beckons her over.*)

LADY AGATHA. Yes, Mamma!

DUCHESS OF BERWICK (*aside*). Did Mr. Hopper definitely—

LADY AGATHA. Yes, Mamma.

DUCHESS OF BERWICK. And what answer did you give him, dear child?

LADY AGATHA. Yes, Mamma.

DUCHESS OF BERWICK (*affectionately*). My dear one!
You always say the right thing. Mr. Hopper! James!
Agatha has told me everything. How cleverly you have
both kept your secret.

HOPPER. You don't mind my taking Agatha off to
Australia, then, Duchess?

DUCHESS OF BERWICK (*indignantly*). To Australia?
Oh, don't mention that dreadful, vulgar place.

HOPPER. But she said she'd like to come with me.

DUCHESS OF BERWICK (*severely*). Did you say that,
Agatha?

LADY AGATHA. Yes, Mamma.

DUCHESS OF BERWICK. Agatha, you say the most silly
things possible. I think on the whole that Grosvenor
Square would be a more healthy place to reside in. There
are lots of vulgar people who live in Grosvenor Square,
but at any rate there are no horrid kangaroos crawling
about. But we'll talk about that to-morrow. James, you
can take Agatha down. You'll come to lunch, of course,
James. At half-past one instead of two. The Duke will
wish to say a few words to you, I am sure.

HOPPER. I should like to have a chat with the Duke,
Duchess. He has not said a single word to me yet.

DUCHESS OF BERWICK. I think you'll find he will have
a great deal to say to you to-morrow. (*Exit* LADY AGATHA
with MR. HOPPER.) And now good-night, Margaret. I'm
afraid it's the old, old story, dear. Love—well, not love at
first sight, but love at the end of the season, which is so
much more satisfactory.

LADY WINDERMERE. Good-night, Duchess.

(*Exit the* DUCHESS OF BERWICK *on* LORD PLYMDALE'S
arm.)

LADY PLYMDALE. My dear Margaret, what a handsome woman your husband has been dancing with!

I should be quite jealous if I were you! Is she a great friend of yours?

LADY WINDERMERE. No!

LADY PLYMDALE. Really? Good-night, dear. (*Looks at* MR. DUMBY *and exits.*)

DUMBY. Awful manners young Hopper has!

CECIL GRAHAM. Ah! Hopper is one of Nature's gentlemen, the worst type of gentleman I know.

DUMBY. Sensible woman, Lady Windermere. Lots of wives would have objected to Mrs. Erlynne coming. But Lady Windermere has that uncommon thing called common sense.

CECIL GRAHAM. And Windermere knows that nothing looks so like innocence as an indiscretion.

DUMBY. Yes; dear Windermere is becoming almost modern. Never thought he would. (*Bows to* LADY WINDERMERE *and exits.*)

LADY JEDBURGH. Good-night, Lady Windermere. What a fascinating woman Mrs. Erlynne is! She is coming to lunch on Thursday. Won't you come too? I expect the Bishop and dear Lady Merton.

LADY WINDERMERE. I am afraid I am engaged, Lady Jedburgh.

LADY JEDBURGH. So sorry. Come, dear.

(*Exeunt* LADY JEDBURGH *and* Miss GRAHAM.)

(*Enter* MRS. ERLYNNE *and* LORD WINDERMERE.)

MRS. ERLYNNE. Charming ball it has been! Quite reminds me of old days. (*Sits on the sofa.*) And I see that there are just as many fools in society as there used to be. So pleased to find that nothing has altered! Except Margaret. She's grown quite pretty. The last time I saw her—twenty years ago, she was a fright in flannel. Positive fright, I assure you. The dear Duchess! and that sweet Lady Agatha! Just the type of girl I like! Well, really, Windermere, if I am to be the Duchess's sister-in-law——

LORD WINDERMERE (sitting L. *of her*). But are you——

(*Exit* MR. CECIL GRAHAM *with rest of guests.* LADY WINDERMERE *watches with a look of scorn and pain* MRS. ERLYNNE *and her husband. They are unconscious of her presence.*)

MRS. ERLYNNE. Oh, yes! He's to call to-morrow at twelve o'clock. He wanted to propose to-night. In fact he did. He kept on proposing. Poor Augustus, you know how he repeats himself. Such a bad habit! But I told him I wouldn't give him an answer till to-morrow. Of course I am going to take him. And I dare say I'll make him an admirable wife, as wives go. And there is a great deal of good in Lord Augustus. Fortunately it is all on the surface. Just where good qualities should be. Of course you must help me in this matter.

LORD WINDERMERE. I am not called on to encourage Lord Augustus, I suppose?

MRS. ERLYNNE. Oh, no! I do the encouraging. But you will make me a handsome settlement, Windermere, won't you?

LORD WINDERMERE (*frowning*). Is that what you want to talk to me about to-night?

MRS. ERLYNNE. Yes.

LORD WINDERMERE (*with a gesture of impatience*). I will not talk of it here.

MRS. ERLYNNE (*laughing*). Then we will talk of it on the terrace. Even business should have a picturesque background. Should it not, Windermere? With a proper background women can do anything.

LORD WINDERMERE. Won't to-morrow do as well?

MRS. ERLYNNE. No; you see, to-morrow I am going to accept him. And I think it would be a good thing if I was

able to tell him that—well, what shall I say?—£2,000
a year left to me by a third cousin—or a second husband—or some distant relative of that kind. It would
be an additional attraction, wouldn't it? You have a delightful opportunity now of paying me a compliment,
Windermere. But you are not very clever at paying compliments. I am afraid Margaret doesn't encourage you
in that excellent habit. It's a great mistake on her part.
When men give up saying what is charming, they give
up thinking what is charming. But seriously, what do you
say to £2,000? £2,500, I think. In modern life margin is
everything. Windermere, don't you think the world an
intensely amusing place? I do!

(*Exit on terrace with* LORD WINDERMERE. *Music strikes
up in ballroom.*)

LADY WINDERMERE. To stay in this house any longer
is impossible. To-night a man who loves me offered me
his whole life. I refused it. It was foolish of me. I will offer him mine now. I will give him mine. I will go to him!
(*Puts on cloak and goes to door, then turns back. Sits
down at table and writes a letter, puts it into an envelope,
and leaves it on table.*) Arthur has never understood me.
When he reads this he will. He may do as he chooses
now with his life. I have done with mine as I think best,
as I think right. It is he who has broken the bond of
marriage—not I. I only break its bondage.

(*Exit.*)

(PARKER *enters* L. *and crosses towards the ballroom* R.
Enter MRS. ERLYNNE.)

MRS. ERLYNNE. Is Lady Windermere in the ballroom?
PARKER. Her ladyship has just gone out.
MRS. ERLYNNE. Gone out? She's not on the terrace?

PARKER. No, madam. Her ladyship has just gone out of the house.

MRS. ERLYNNE (*starts, and looks at the servant with a puzzled expression on her face*). Out of the house?

PARKER. Yes, madam—her ladyship told me she had left a letter for his lordship on the table.

MRS. ERLYNNE. A letter for Lord Windermere?

PARKER. Yes, madam.

MRS. ERLYNNE. Thank you. (*Exit* PARKER. *The music in the ballroom stops.*) Gone out of her house! A letter addressed to her husband! (*Goes over to bureau and looks at letter. Takes it up and lays it down again with a shudder of fear.*) No, no! It would be impossible! Life doesn't repeat its tragedies like that! Oh, why does this horrible fancy come across me? Why do I remember now the one moment of my life I most wish to forget? Does life repeat its tragedies? (*Tears letter open and reads it, then sinks down into a chair with a gesture of anguish.*) Oh, how terrible! The same words that twenty years ago I wrote to her father! and how bitterly I have been punished for it! No; my punishment, my real punishment is to-night, is now! (*Still seated* R.)

(*Enter* WINDERMERE L. U. E.)

LORD WINDERMERE. Have you said good-night to my wife? (*Comes* C.)

MRS. ERLYNNE (*crushing letter in her hand*). Yes.

LORD WINDERMERE. Where is she?

MRS. ERLYNNE. She is very tired. She has gone to bed. She said she had a headache.

LORD WINDERMERE. I must go to her. You'll excuse me?

MRS. ERLYNNE (*rising hurriedly*). Oh, no! It's nothing serious. She's only very tired, that is all. Besides, there are people still in the supper-room. She wants you to make her apologies to them. She said she didn't wish to be disturbed. (*Drops letter.*) She asked me to tell you.

LORD WINDERMERE (*picks up letter*). You have dropped something.

MRS. ERLYNNE. Oh, yes, thank you, that is mine. (*Puts out her hand to take it.*)

LORD WINDERMERE (*still looking at letter*). But it's my wife's handwriting, isn't it?

MRS. ERLYNNE (*takes the letter quickly*). Yes, it's—an address. Will you ask them to call my carriage, please?

LORD WINDERMERE. Certainly. (*Goes L. and exits.*)

MRS. ERLYNNE. Thanks. What can I do? What can I do? I feel a passion awakening within me that I never felt before. What can it mean? The daughter must not be like the mother—that would be terrible. How can I save her? How can I save my child? A moment may ruin a life. Who knows that better than I? Windermere must be got out of the house; that is absolutely necessary. (*Goes L.*) But how shall I do it? It must be done somehow. Ah!

(*Enter* LORD AUGUSTUS R. U. E., *carrying bouquet.*)

LORD AUGUSTUS. Dear lady, I am in such suspense! May I have an answer to my request?

MRS. ERLYNNE. Lord Augustus, listen to me. You are to take Lord Windermere down to your club at once, and keep him there as long as possible. You understand?

LORD AUGUSTUS. But you said you wished me to keep early hours!

MRS. ERLYNNE (*nervously*). Do what I tell you. Do what I tell you.

LORD AUGUSTUS. And my reward?

MRS. ERLYNNE. Your reward? Your reward? Oh! ask me that to-morrow. But don't let Windermere out of your sight to-night. If you do I will never forgive you. I will never speak to you again. I'll have nothing to do with you. Remember, you are to keep Windermere at your club, and don't let him come back to-night.

(*Exit.*)

LORD AUGUSTUS. Well, really, I might be her husband already. Positively I might. (*Follows her in a bewildered manner.*)

CURTAIN

ACT III

SCENE.—LORD DARLINGTON'S *rooms. A large sofa is in front of fireplace* R. *At the back of the stage a curtain is drawn across the window. Doors* L. *and* R. *Table* R. *with writing materials. Table* C. *with syphons, glasses, and Tantalus frame. Table* L. *with cigar and cigarette box. Lamps lit.*

LADY WINDERMERE (*standing by the fireplace*). Why doesn't he come? This waiting is horrible. He should be here. Why is he not here, to wake by passionate words some fire within me? I am cold—cold as a loveless thing. Arthur must have read my letter by this time. If he cared for me, he would have come after me, would have taken me back by force. But he doesn't care. He's entrammeled by this woman—fascinated by her—dominated by her. If a woman wants to hold a man, she has merely to appeal to what is worst in him. We make gods of men, and they leave us. Others make brutes of them and they fawn and are faithful. How hideous life is! . . . Oh! it was mad of me to come here, horribly mad. And yet which is the worst, I wonder, to be at the mercy of a man who loves one, or the wife of a man who in one's own house dishonours one? What woman knows? What woman in the whole world? But will he love me always, this man to whom I am giving my life? What do I bring him? Lips that have lost the note of joy, eyes that are blighted by tears, chill hands and icy heart. I bring him nothing. I must go back—no; I can't go back, my letter has put me in their power—Arthur would not take me back! That fatal letter! No! Lord Darlington leaves England to-morrow. I will go with him—I have no choice. (*Sits down for a few moments. Then starts up and puts on her cloak.*) No, no! I will go back, let Arthur do with me what he pleases. I can't wait here. It has been madness, my coming. I must go at once. As for Lord Darlington—Oh, here he is! What shall I do? What can I say to him? Will he let me go away at all? I have heard that men are brutal, horrible. . . . Oh! (*Hides her face in her hands.*)

(*Enter* MRS. ERLYNNE L.)

MRS. ERLYNNE. Lady Windermere! (LADY WINDERMERE *starts and looks up. Then recoils in contempt.*) Thank Heaven I am in time. You must go back to your husband's house immediately.

LADY WINDERMERE. Must?

MRS. ERLYNNE (*authoritatively*). Yes, you must! There is not a second to be lost. Lord Darlington may return at any moment.

LADY WINDERMERE. Don't come near me.

MRS. ERLYNNE. Oh, you are on the brink of ruin: you are on the brink of a hideous precipice. You must leave this place at once. My carriage is waiting at the corner of the street. You must come with me and drive straight home. (LADY WINDERMERE *throws off her cloak and flings it on the sofa.*) What are you doing?

LADY WINDERMERE. Mrs. Erlynne—if you had not come here, I would have gone back. But now that I see you, I feel that nothing in the whole world would induce

me to live under the same roof as Lord Windermere.
You fill me with horror. There is something about you
that stirs the wildest rage within me. And I know why
you are here. My husband sent you to lure me back that
I might serve as a blind to whatever relations exist between you and him.

MRS. ERLYNNE. Oh! you don't think that—you can't.

LADY WINDERMERE. Go back to my husband, Mrs. Erlynne. He belongs to you and not to me. I suppose he
is afraid of a scandal. Men are such cowards. They outrage every law of the world, and are afraid of the world's
tongue. But he had better prepare himself. He shall have
a scandal. He shall have the worst scandal there has
been in London for years. He shall see his name in every
vile paper, mine on every hideous placard.

MRS. ERLYNNE. No—no——

LADY WINDERMERE. Yes, he shall! Had he come himself, I admit I would have gone back to the life of degradation you and he had prepared for me—I was going
back—but to stay himself at home, and to send you as
his messenger—oh! it was infamous—infamous!

MRS. ERLYNNE (C.). Lady Windermere, you wrong me
horribly—you wrong your husband horribly. He doesn't
know you are here—he thinks you are safe in your own
house. He thinks you are asleep in your own room. He
never read the mad letter you wrote to him!

LADY WINDERMERE (R.). Never read it!

MRS. ERLYNNE. No—he knows nothing about it.

LADY WINDERMERE. How simple you think me! (Going to her.) You are lying to me!

MRS. ERLYNNE (restraining herself). I am not. I am
telling you the truth.

LADY WINDERMERE. If my husband didn't read my letter, how is it that you are here? Who told you I had left
the house you were shameless enough to enter? Who
told you where I had gone to? My husband told you, and
sent you to decoy me back. (Crosses L.)

MRS. ERLYNNE (R. C.). Your husband has never seen the letter. I—saw it, I opened it. I—read it.

LADY WINDERMERE (*turning to her*). You opened a letter of mine to my husband? You wouldn't dare!

MRS. ERLYNNE. Dare! Oh! to save you from the abyss into which you are falling, there is nothing in the world I would not dare, nothing in the whole world. Here is the letter. Your husband has never read it. He never shall read it. (*Going to fireplace.*) It should never have been written. (*Tears it and throws it into the fire.*)

LADY WINDERMERE (*with infinite contempt in her voice and look*). How do I know that that was my letter after all? You seem to think the commonest device can take me in!

MRS. ERLYNNE. Oh! why do you disbelieve everything I tell you! What object do you think I have in coming here, except to save you from utter ruin, to save you from the consequence of a hideous mistake? That letter that is burning now *was* your letter. I swear it to you!

LADY WINDERMERE (*slowly*). You took good care to burn it before I had examined it. I cannot trust you. You, whose whole life is a lie, how could you speak the truth about anything? (*Sits down.*)

MRS. ERLYNNE (*hurriedly*). Think as you like about me—say what you choose against me, but go back, go back to the husband you love.

LADY WINDERMERE (*sullenly*). I do *not* love him!

MRS. ERLYNNE. You do, and you know that he loves you.

LADY WINDERMERE. He does not understand what love is. He understands it as little as you do—but I see what you want. It would be a great advantage for you to get me back. Dear Heaven! what a life I would have then! Living at the mercy of a woman who has neither mercy nor pity in her, a woman whom it is an infamy to meet, a degradation to know, a vile woman, a woman who comes between husband and wife!

MRS. ERLYNNE (*with a gesture of despair*). Lady Windermere, Lady Windermere, don't say such terrible things. You don't know how terrible they are, how terrible and how unjust. Listen, you must listen! Only go back to your husband, and I promise you never to communicate with him again on any pretext—never to see him—never to have anything to do with his life or yours. The money that he gave me, he gave me not through love, but through hatred, not in worship, but in contempt. The hold I have over him——

LADY WINDERMERE (*rising*). Ah! you admit you have a hold!

MRS. ERLYNNE. Yes, and I will tell you what it is. It is his love for you, Lady Windermere.

LADY WINDERMERE. You expect me to believe that?

MRS. ERLYNNE. You must believe it! It is true. It is his love for you that has made him submit to—oh! call it what you like, tyranny, threats, anything you choose. But it is his love for you. His desire to spare you shame, yes, shame and disgrace.

LADY WINDERMERE. What do you mean? You are insolent! What have I to do with you?

MRS. ERLYNNE (*humbly*). Nothing. I know it—but I tell you that your husband loves you——that you may never meet with such love again in your whole life—that such love you will never meet—and that if you throw it away, the day may come when you will starve for love and it will not be given to you, beg for love and it will be denied you——Oh! Arthur loves you!

LADY WINDERMERE. Arthur? And you tell me there is nothing between you?

MRS. ERLYNNE. Lady Windermere, before Heaven your husband is guiltless of all offense towards you! And I—I tell you that had it ever occurred to me that such a monstrous suspicion would have entered your mind, I would have died rather than have crossed your life or his—oh! died, gladly died! (*Moves away to sofa* R.)

LADY WINDERMERE. You talk as if you had a heart. Women like you have no hearts. Heart is not in you. You are bought and sold. (*Sits* L. C.)

MRS. ERLYNNE (*starts, with a gesture of pain. Then restrains herself, and comes over to where* LADY WINDERMERE *is sitting. As she speaks, she stretches out her hands towards her, but does not dare to touch her*). Believe what you choose about me. I am not worth a moment's sorrow. But don't spoil your beautiful young life on my account! You don't know what may be in store for you, unless you leave this house at once. You don't know what it is to fall into the pit, to be despised, mocked, abandoned, sneered at—to be an outcast! to find the door shut against one, to have to creep in by hideous byways, afraid every moment lest the mask should be stripped from one's face, and all the while to hear the laughter, the horrible laughter of the world, a thing more tragic than all the tears the world has ever shed. You don't know what it is. One pays for one's sin, and then one pays again, and all one's life one pays. You must never know that.—As for me, if suffering be an expiation, then at this moment I have expiated all my faults, whatever they have been; for to-night you have made a heart in one who had it not, made it and broken it.—But let that pass. I may have wrecked my own life, but I will not let you wreck yours. You—why, you are a mere girl, you would be lost. You haven't got the kind of brain that enables a woman to get back. You have neither the wit nor the courage. You couldn't stand dishonour. No! Go back, Lady Windermere, to the husband who loves you, whom you love. You have a child, Lady Windermere. Go back to that child who even now, in pain or in joy, may be calling to you. (LADY WINDERMERE *rises.*) God gave you that child. He will require from you that you make his life fine, that you watch over him. What answer will you make to God if his life is ruined through you? Back to your house, Lady Windermere—your husband loves you. He has never swerved for a moment from the love he bears you. But even if he had a thousand loves, you must stay with your child. If he was harsh to you, you must stay with your child. If he ill-treated you, you must stay with your child. If he abandoned you, your place is with your child. (LADY WINDERMERE *bursts into tears and buries her face in her hands.*) (*Rushing to her.*) Lady Windermere!

LADY WINDERMERE (*holding out her hands to her, helplessly, as a child might do*). Take me home. Take me home.

MRS. ERLYNNE (*is about to embrace her. Then restrains herself. There is a look of wonderful joy in her face*). Come! Where is your cloak? (*Getting it from sofa.*) Here. Put it on. Come at once! (*They go to the door.*)

LADY WINDERMERE. Stop! Don't you hear voices?

MRS. ERLYNNE. No, no. There is no one.

LADY WINDERMERE. Yes, there is! Listen! Oh, that is my husband's voice! He is coming in! Save me! Oh, it's some plot! You have sent for him! (*Voices outside.*)

MRS. ERLYNNE. Silence! I am here to save you if I can. But I fear it is too late! There! (*Points to the curtain across the window.*) The first chance you have, slip out, if you ever get a chance!

LADY WINDERMERE. But you!

MRS. ERLYNNE. Oh, never mind me. I'll face them. (LADY WINDERMERE *hides herself behind the curtain.*)

LORD AUGUSTUS (*outside*). Nonsense, dear Windermere, you must not leave me!

MRS. ERLYNNE. Lord Augustus! Then it is I who am lost! (*Hesitates for a moment, then looks round and sees door R., and exits through it.*)

(*Enter* LORD DARLINGTON, MR. DUMBY, LORD WINDERMERE, LORD AUGUSTUS LORTON, *and* MR. CECIL GRAHAM.)

DUMBY. What a nuisance their turning us out of the club at this hour! It's only two o'clock. (*Sinks into a chair.*) The lively part of the evening is only just beginning. (*Yawns and closes his eyes.*)

LORD WINDERMERE. It is very good of you, Lord Darlington, allowing Augustus to force our company on you, but I'm afraid I can't stay long.

LORD DARLINGTON. Really! I am so sorry! You'll take a cigar, won't you?

LORD WINDERMERE. Thanks! (*Sits down.*)

LORD AUGUSTUS (*to* LORD WINDERMERE). My dear boy, you must not dream of going. I have a great deal to talk to you about of demmed importance, too. (*Sits down with him at* L. *table.*)

CECIL GRAHAM. Oh, we all know what that is! Tuppy can't talk about anything but Mrs. Erlynne!

LORD WINDERMERE. Well, that is no business of yours, is it, Cecil?

CECIL GRAHAM. None. That is why it interests me. My own business always bores me to death. I prefer other people's.

LORD DARLINGTON. Have something to drink, you fellows. Cecil, you'll have a whisky and soda?

CECIL GRAHAM. Thanks. (*Goes to the table with* LORD DARLINGTON.) Mrs. Erlynne looked very handsome tonight, didn't she?

LORD DARLINGTON. I am not one of her admirers.

CECIL GRAHAM. I usedn't to be, but I am now. Why, she actually made me introduce her to poor dear Aunt Caroline. I believe she is going to lunch there.

LORD DARLINGTON (*in surprise*). No?

CECIL GRAHAM. She is, really.

LORD DARLINGTON. Excuse me, you fellows. I'm going away to-morrow. And I have to write a few letters. (*Goes to writing table and sits down.*)

DUMBY. Clever woman, Mrs. Erlynne.

CECIL GRAHAM. Hallo, Dumby! I thought you were asleep.

DUMBY. I am, I usually am!

LORD AUGUSTUS. A very clever woman. Knows perfectly well what a demmed fool I am—knows it as well as I do myself. (CECIL GRAHAM *comes towards him, laughing*). Ah! you may laugh, my boy, but it is a great thing to come across a woman who thoroughly understands one.

DUMBY. It is an awfully dangerous thing. They always end by marrying one.

CECIL GRAHAM. But I thought, Tuppy, you were never going to see her again. Yes, you told me so yesterday evening at the club. You said you'd heard——(*Whispering to him.*)

LORD AUGUSTUS. Oh, she's explained that.

CECIL GRAHAM. And the Wiesbaden affair?

LORD AUGUSTUS. She's explained that, too.

DUMBY. And her income, Tuppy? Has she explained that?

LORD AUGUSTUS (*in a very serious voice*). She's going to explain that to-morrow. (CECIL GRAHAM *goes back to* C. *table.*)

DUMBY. Awfully commercial, women now-a-days. Our grandmothers threw their caps over the mills, of course, but, by Jove, their granddaughters only throw their caps over mills that can raise the wind for them.

LORD AUGUSTUS. You want to make her out a wicked woman. She is not!

CECIL GRAHAM. Oh! Wicked women bother one. Good women bore one. That is the only difference between them.

LORD DARLINGTON (*puffing a cigar*). Mrs. Erlynne has a future before her.

DUMBY. Mrs. Erlynne has a past before her.

LORD AUGUSTUS. I prefer women with a past. They're always so demmed amusing to talk to.

CECIL GRAHAM. Well, you'll have lots of topics of conversation with *her,* Tuppy. (*Rising and going to him.*)

LORD AUGUSTUS. You're getting annoying, dear boy; you're getting demmed annoying.

CECIL GRAHAM (*puts his hands on his shoulders*). Now, Tuppy, you've lost your figure and you've lost your character. Don't lose your temper; you have only got one.

LORD AUGUSTUS. My dear boy, if I wasn't the most good-natured man in London——

CECIL GRAHAM. We'd treat you with more respect, wouldn't we, Tuppy? (*Strolls away.*)

DUMBY. The youth of the present day are quite monstrous. They have absolutely no respect for dyed hair. (LORD AUGUSTUS *looks round angrily.*)

CECIL GRAHAM. Mrs. Erlynne has a very great respect for dear Tuppy.

DUMBY. Then Mrs. Erlynne sets an admirable example to the rest of her sex. It is perfectly brutal the way most women now-a-days behave to men who are not their husbands.

LORD WINDERMERE. Dumby, you are ridiculous, and, Cecil, you let your tongue run away with you. You must leave Mrs. Erlynne alone. You don't really know anything about her, and you're always talking scandal against her.

CECIL GRAHAM (*coming towards him* L. C.). My dear Arthur, *I* never talk scandal. *I* only talk gossip.

LORD WINDERMERE. What is the difference between scandal and gossip?

CECIL GRAHAM. Oh, gossip is charming! History is merely gossip. But scandal is gossip made tedious by morality. Now I never moralize. A man who moralizes is usually a hypocrite, and a woman who moralizes is invariably plain. There is nothing in the whole world so unbecoming to a woman as a Nonconformist conscience. And most women know it, I'm glad to say.

LORD AUGUSTUS. Just my sentiments, dear boy, just my sentiments.

CECIL GRAHAM. Sorry to hear it, Tuppy; whenever people agree with me, I always feel I must be wrong.

LORD AUGUSTUS. My dear boy, when I was your age——

CECIL GRAHAM. But you never were, Tuppy, and you never will be. (*Goes up* C.) I say, Darlington, let us have some cards. You'll play, Arthur, won't you?

LORD WINDERMERE. No, thanks, Cecil.

DUMBY (*with a sigh*). Good heavens! how marriage ruins a man. It's as demoralizing as cigarettes, and far more expensive.

CECIL GRAHAM. You'll play, of course, Tuppy?

LORD AUGUSTUS (*pouring himself out a brandy and soda at table*). Can't, dear boy. Promised Mrs. Erlynne never to play or drink again.

CECIL GRAHAM. Now, my dear Tuppy, don't be led astray into the paths of virtue. Reformed, you would be perfectly tedious. That is the worst of women. They always want one to be good. And if we are good, when they meet us, they don't love us at all. They like to find us quite irretrievably bad, and to leave us quite unattractively good.

LORD DARLINGTON (*rising from* R. *table, where he has been writing letters*). They always do find us bad!

DUMBY. I don't think we are bad. I think we are all good except Tuppy.

LORD DARLINGTON. No, we are all in the gutter, but some of us are looking at the stars. (*Sits down at* C. *table.*)

DUMBY. We are all in the gutter, but some of us are looking at the stars? Upon my word, you are very romantic tonight, Darlington.

CECIL GRAHAM. Too romantic! You must be in love. Who is the girl?

LORD DARLINGTON. The woman I love is not free, or

thinks she isn't. (*Glances instinctively at* LORD WINDER-
MERE *while he speaks.*)

CECIL GRAHAM. A married woman, then! Well, there's
nothing in the world like the devotion of a married
woman. It's a thing no married man knows anything
about.

LORD DARLINGTON. Oh, she doesn't love me. She is a
good woman. She is the only good woman I have ever
met in my life.

CECIL GRAHAM. The only good woman you have ever
met in your life?

LORD DARLINGTON. Yes.

CECIL GRAHAM (*lighting a cigarette*). Well, you are a
lucky fellow! Why, I have met hundreds of good women.
I never seem to meet any but good women. The world is
perfectly packed with good women. To know them is a
middle-class education.

LORD DARLINGTON. This woman has purity and innocence. She has everything we men have not.

CECIL GRAHAM. My dear fellow, what on earth should
we men do going about with purity and innocence? A
carefully thought-out buttonhole is much more effective.

DUMBY. She doesn't really love you, then?

LORD DARLINGTON. No, she does not!

DUMBY. I congratulate you, my dear fellow. In this
world there are only two tragedies. One is not getting
what one wants, and the other is getting it. The last is
much the worst, the last is a real tragedy! But I am interested to hear she does not love you. How long could you
love a woman who didn't love you, Cecil?

CECIL GRAHAM. A woman who didn't love me? Oh,
all my life!

DUMBY. So could I. But it's so difficult to meet one.

LORD DARLINGTON. How can you be so conceited,
Dumby?

DUMBY. I didn't say it as a matter of conceit. I said it
as a matter of regret. I have been wildly, madly adored.

I am sorry I have. It has been an immense nuisance. I should like to be allowed a little time to myself now and then.

LORD AUGUSTUS (*looking round*). Time to educate yourself, I suppose.

DUMBY. No, time to forget all I have learned. That is much more important, dear Tuppy. (LORD AUGUSTUS *moves uneasily in his chair.*)

LORD DARLINGTON. What cynics you fellows are!

CECIL GRAHAM. What is a cynic? (*Sitting on the back of the sofa.*)

LORD DARLINGTON. A man who knows the price of everything, and the value of nothing.

CECIL GRAHAM. And a sentimentalist, my dear Darlington, is a man who sees an absurd value in everything and doesn't know the market price of any single thing.

LORD DARLINGTON. You always amuse me, Cecil. You talk as if you were a man of experience.

CECIL GRAHAM. I am. (*Moves up to front of fireplace.*)

LORD DARLINGTON. You are far too young!

CECIL GRAHAM. That is a great error. Experience is a question of instinct about life. I have got it. Tuppy hasn't. Experience is the name Tuppy gives to his mistakes. That is all. (LORD AUGUSTUS *looks round indignantly.*)

DUMBY. Experience is the name everyone gives to their mistakes.

CECIL GRAHAM (*standing with his back to fireplace*). One shouldn't commit any. (*Sees* LADY WINDERMERE'*s fan on sofa.*)

DUMBY. Life would be very dull without them.

CECIL GRAHAM. Of course you are quite faithful to this woman you are in love with, Darlington, to this good woman?

LORD DARLINGTON. Cecil, if one really loves a woman, all other women in the world become absolutely meaningless to one. Love changes one—I am changed.

CECIL GRAHAM. Dear me! How very interesting!

Tuppy, I want to talk to you. (LORD AUGUSTUS *takes no notice.*)

DUMBY. It's no use talking to Tuppy. You might just as well talk to a brick wall.

CECIL GRAHAM. But I like talking to a brick wall—it's the only thing in the world that never contradicts me! Tuppy!

LORD AUGUSTUS. Well, what is it? What is it? (*Rising and going over to* CECIL GRAHAM.)

CECIL GRAHAM. Come over here. I want you particularly. (*Aside.*) Darlington has been moralizing and talking about the purity of love, and that sort of thing, and he has got some woman in his rooms all the time.

LORD AUGUSTUS. No, really! really!

CECIL GRAHAM (*in a low voice*). Yes, here is her fan. (*Points to the fan.*)

LORD AUGUSTUS (*chuckling*). By Jove! By Jove!

LORD WINDERMERE (UP *by door*). I am really off now, Lord Darlington. I am sorry you are leaving England so soon. Pray call on us when you come back! My wife and I will be charmed to see you!

LORD DARLINGTON (UP *stage with* LORD WINDERMERE). I am afraid I shall be away for many years. Good-night.

CECIL GRAHAM. Arthur!

LORD WINDERMERE. What?

CECIL GRAHAM. I want to speak to you for a moment. No, do come!

LORD WINDERMERE (*putting on his coat*). I can't—I'm off!

CECIL GRAHAM. It is something very particular. It will interest you enormously.

LORD WINDERMERE (*smiling*). It is some of your nonsense, Cecil.

CECIL GRAHAM. It isn't! It isn't really!

LORD AUGUSTUS (*going to him*). My dear fellow, you mustn't go yet. I have a lot to talk to you about. And Cecil has something to show you.

LORD WINDERMERE (*walking over*). Well, what is it?

CECIL GRAHAM. Darlington has got a woman here in his rooms. Here is her fan. Amusing, isn't it? (*A pause.*)

LORD WINDERMERE. Good God! (*Seizes the fan— DUMBY rises.*)

CECIL GRAHAM. What is the matter?

LORD WINDERMERE. Lord Darlington!

LORD DARLINGTON (*turning round*). Yes!

LORD WINDERMERE. What is my wife's fan doing here in your rooms? Hands off, Cecil! Don't touch me!

LORD DARLINGTON. Your wife's fan?

LORD WINDERMERE. Yes, here it is!

LORD DARLINGTON (*walking towards him*). I don't know!

LORD WINDERMERE. You must know. I demand an explanation! Don't hold me, you fool! (*To* CECIL GRAHAM.)

LORD DARLINGTON (*aside*). She is here, after all!

LORD WINDERMERE. Speak, sir! Why is my wife's fan here? Answer me, by God! I'll search your rooms, and if my wife's here, I'll—— (*Moves.*)

LORD DARLINGTON. You shall not search my rooms. You have no right to do so. I forbid you!

LORD WINDERMERE. You scoundrel! I'll not leave your room till I have searched every corner of it! What moves behind that curtain? (*Rushes towards curtain* C.)

MRS. ERLYNNE (*enters behind* R.). Lord Windermere!

LORD WINDERMERE. Mrs. Erlynne! (*Every one starts and turns round.* LADY WINDERMERE *slips out from behind the curtain and glides from the room* L.)

MRS. ERLYNNE. I am afraid I took your wife's fan in mistake for my own, when I was leaving your house tonight. I am so sorry. (*Takes fan from him.* LORD WINDERMERE *looks at her in contempt,* LORD DARLINGTON *in mingled astonishment and anger.* LORD AUGUSTUS *turns away. The other men smile at each other.*)

CURTAIN

ACT IV

SCENE.—*Same as in* Act I.

Lady Windermere (*lying on sofa*). How can I tell him? I can't tell him. It would kill me. I wonder what happened after I escaped from that horrible room. Perhaps she told them the true reason of her being there, and the real meaning of that—fatal fan of mine. Oh, if he knows—how can I look him in the face again! He would never forgive me. (*Touches bell.*) How securely one thinks one lives—out of reach of temptation, sin, folly. And then suddenly—— Oh! Life is terrible. It rules us, we do not rule it.

(*Enter* Rosalie r.)

Rosalie. Did your ladyship ring for me?

Lady Windermere. Yes. Have you found out at what time Lord Windermere came in last night?

Rosalie. His lordship did not come in till five o'clock.

Lady Windermere. Five o'clock! He knocked at my door this morning, didn't he?

Rosalie. Yes, my lady—at half-past nine. I told him your ladyship was not awake yet.

Lady Windermere. Did he say anything?

Rosalie. Something about your ladyship's fan. I didn't quite catch what his lordship said. Has the fan been lost, my lady? I can't find it, and Parker says it was not left in any of the rooms. He has looked in all of them and on the terrace as well.

Lady Windermere. It doesn't matter. Tell Parker not to trouble. That will do. (*Exit* Rosalie.)

Lady Windermere (*rising*). She is sure to tell him. I can fancy a person doing a wonderful act of self-sacrifice, doing it spontaneously, recklessly, nobly—and afterwards finding out that it costs too much. Why should she hesitate between her ruin and mine? ... How strange! I would have publicly disgraced her in my own house. She accepts public disgrace in the house of another to save me. ... There is a bitter irony in things, a bitter irony in the way we talk of good and bad women. ... Oh, what a lesson! and what a pity that in life we only get our lessons when they are of no use to us! For even if she doesn't tell, I must. Oh! the shame of it, the shame of it! To tell it is to live through it all again. Actions are the first tragedy in life, words are the second. Words are perhaps the worst. Words are merciless. ... Oh! (*Starts as* LORD WINDERMERE *enters.*)

LORD WINDERMERE (*kisses her*). Margaret—how pale you look!

LADY WINDERMERE. I slept very badly.

LORD WINDERMERE (*sitting on sofa with her*). I am so sorry. I came in dreadfully late, and didn't like to wake you. You are crying, dear.

LADY WINDERMERE. Yes, I am crying, for I have something to tell you, Arthur.

LORD WINDERMERE. My dear child, you are not well. You've been doing too much. Let us go away to the country. You'll be all right at Selby. The season is almost over. There is no use staying on. Poor darling! We'll go away to-day, if you like. (*Rises.*) We can easily catch the 4:30. I'll send a wire to Fannen. (*Crosses and sits down at table to write a telegram.*)

LADY WINDERMERE. Yes, let us go away to-day. No, I can't go to-day, Arthur. There is some one I must see before I leave town—some one who has been kind to me.

LORD WINDERMERE (*rising and leaning over sofa*). Kind to you?

LADY WINDERMERE. Far more than that. (*Rises and goes to him.*) I will tell you, Arthur, but only love me, love me as you used to love me.

LORD WINDERMERE. Used to? You are not thinking of

that wretched woman who came here last night? (*Coming round and sitting* R. *of her.*) You don't still imagine—no, you couldn't.

LADY WINDERMERE. I don't. I know now I was wrong and foolish.

LORD WINDERMERE. It was very good of you to receive her last night—but you are never to see her again.

LADY WINDERMERE. Why do you say that? (*A pause.*)

LORD WINDERMERE (*holding her hand*). Margaret, I thought Mrs. Erlynne was a woman more sinned against than sinning, as the phrase goes. I thought she wanted to be good, to get back into a place that she had lost by a moment's folly, to lead again a decent life. I believed what she told me—I was mistaken in her. She is bad—as bad as a woman can be.

LADY WINDERMERE. Arthur, Arthur, don't talk so bitterly about any woman. I don't think now that people can be divided into the good and the bad, as though they were two separate races or creations. What are called good women may have terrible things in them, mad moods of recklessness, assertion, jealousy, sin. Bad women, as they are termed, may have in them sorrow, repentance, pity, sacrifice. And I don't think Mrs. Erlynne a bad woman—I know she's not.

LORD WINDERMERE. My dear child, the woman's impossible. No matter what harm she tries to do us, you must never see her again. She is inadmissible anywhere.

LADY WINDERMERE. But I want to see her. I want her to come here.

LORD WINDERMERE. Never!

LADY WINDERMERE. She came here once as *your* guest. She must come now as *mine*. That is but fair.

LORD WINDERMERE. She should never have come here.

LADY WINDERMERE (*rising*). It is too late, Arthur, to say that now. (*Moves away.*)

LORD WINDERMERE (*rising*). Margaret, if you knew

where Mrs. Erlynne went last night, after she left this house, you would not sit in the same room with her. It was absolutely shameless, the whole thing.

LADY WINDERMERE. Arthur, I can't bear it any longer. I must tell you. Last night——

(*Enter* PARKER *with a tray on which lie* LADY WINDER-MERE's *fan and a card.*)

PARKER. Mrs. Erlynne has called to return your ladyship's fan which she took away by mistake last night. Mrs. Erlynne has written a message on the card.

LADY WINDERMERE. Oh, ask Mrs. Erlynne to be kind enough to come up. (*Reads card.*) Say I shall be very glad to see her. (*Exit* PARKER.) She wants to see me, Arthur.

LORD WINDERMERE (*takes card and looks at it*). Margaret, I *beg* you not to. Let me see her first, at any rate. She's a very dangerous woman. She is the most dangerous woman I know. You don't realize what you're doing.

LADY WINDERMERE. It is right that I should see her.

LORD WINDERMERE. My child, you may be on the brink of a great sorrow. Don't go to meet it. It is absolutely necessary that I should see her before you do.

LADY WINDERMERE. Why should it be necessary?

(*Enter* PARKER.)

PARKER. Mrs. Erlynne.

(*Enter* MRS. ERLYNNE. *Exit* PARKER.)

MRS. ERLYNNE. How do you do, Lady Windermere? (*To* LORD WINDERMERE.) How do you do? Do you know, Lady Windermere, I am so sorry about your fan. I can't imagine how I made such a silly mistake. Most stupid of me. And as I was driving in your direction, I thought I would take the opportunity of returning your property in person, with many apologies for my carelessness, and of bidding you good-bye.

LADY WINDERMERE. Good-bye? (*Moves towards sofa with* MRS. ERLYNNE *and sits down beside her.*) Are you going away, then, Mrs. Erlynne?

MRS. ERLYNNE. Yes; I am going to live abroad again. The English climate doesn't suit me. My—heart is affected here, and that I don't like. I prefer living in the south. London is too full of fogs and—and serious people, Lady Windermere. Whether the fogs produce the serious people or whether the serious people produce the fogs, I don't know, but the whole thing rather gets on my nerves, and so I'm leaving this afternoon by the Club Train.

LADY WINDERMERE. This afternoon? But I wanted so much to come and see you.

MRS. ERLYNNE. How kind of you! But I am afraid I have to go.

LADY WINDERMERE. Shall I never see you again, Mrs. Erlynne?

MRS. ERLYNNE. I am afraid not. Our lives lie too far apart. But there is a little thing I would like you to do for me. I want a photograph of you, Lady Windermere— would you give me one? You don't know how gratified I should be.

LADY WINDERMERE. Oh, with pleasure. There is one on that table. I'll show it to you. (*Goes across to the table.*)

LORD WINDERMERE (*coming up to* MRS. ERLYNNE *and speaking in a low voice*). It is monstrous your intruding yourself here after your conduct last night.

MRS. ERLYNNE (*with an amused smile*). My dear Windermere, manners before morals!

LADY WINDERMERE (*returning*). I'm afraid it is very flattering—I am not so pretty as that. (*Showing photograph.*)

MRS. ERLYNNE. You are much prettier. But haven't you got one of yourself with your little boy?

LADY WINDERMERE. I have. Would you prefer one of those?

MRS. ERLYNNE. Yes.

LADY WINDERMERE. I'll go and get it for you, if you'll excuse me for a moment. I have one upstairs.

MRS. ERLYNNE. So sorry, Lady Windermere, to give you so much trouble.

LADY WINDERMERE (*moves to door* R.). No trouble at all, Mrs. Erlynne.

MRS. ERLYNNE. Thanks so much. (*Exit* LADY WINDERMERE R.) You seem rather out of temper this morning, Windermere. Why should you be? Margaret and I get on charmingly together.

LORD WINDERMERE. I can't bear to see you with her. Besides, you have not told me the truth, Mrs. Erlynne.

MRS. ERLYNNE. I have not told *her* the truth, you mean.

LORD WINDERMERE (*standing* C.). I sometimes wish you had. I should have been spared then the misery, the anxiety, the annoyance of the last six months. But rather than my wife should know—that the mother whom she was taught to consider as dead, the mother whom she has mourned as dead, is living—a divorced woman going about under an assumed name, a bad woman preying upon life, as I know you now to be—rather than that, I was ready to supply you with money to pay bill after bill, extravagance after extravagance, to risk what occurred yesterday, the first quarrel I have ever had with my wife. You don't understand what that means to me. How could you? But I tell you that the only bitter words that ever came from those sweet lips of hers were on your account, and I hate to see you next her. You sully the innocence that is in her. (*Moves* L. C.) And then I used to think that with all your faults you were frank and honest. You are not.

MRS. ERLYNNE. Why do you say that?

LORD WINDERMERE. You made me get you an invitation to my wife's ball.

MRS. ERLYNNE. For my daughter's ball—yes.

LORD WINDERMERE. You came, and within an hour of your leaving the house, you are found in a man's rooms—you are disgraced before everyone. (*Goes* UP *stage* C.)

MRS. ERLYNNE. Yes.

LORD WINDERMERE (*turning round on her*). Therefore I have a right to look upon you as what you are—a worthless, vicious woman. I have the right to tell you never to enter this house, never to attempt to come near my wife——

MRS. ERLYNNE (*coldly*). My daughter, you mean.

LORD WINDERMERE. You have no right to claim her as your daughter. You left her, abandoned her, when she was but a child in the cradle, abandoned her for your lover, who abandoned you in turn.

MRS. ERLYNNE (*rising*). Do you count that to his credit, Lord Windermere—or to mine?

LORD WINDERMERE. To his, now that I know you.

MRS. ERLYNNE. Take care—you had better be careful.

LORD WINDERMERE. Oh, I am not going to mince words for you. I know you thoroughly.

MRS. ERLYNNE (*looking steadily at him*). I question that.

LORD WINDERMERE. I *do* know you. For twenty years of your life you lived without your child, without a thought of your child. One day you read in the papers that she had married a rich man. You saw your hideous chance. You knew that to spare her the ignominy of learning that a woman like you was her mother, I would endure anything. You began your blackmailing.

MRS. ERLYNNE (*shrugging her shoulders*). Don't use ugly words, Windermere. They are vulgar. I saw my chance, it is true, and took it.

LORD WINDERMERE. Yes, you took it—and spoiled it all last night by being found out.

MRS. ERLYNNE (*with a strange smile*). You are quite right, I spoiled it all last night.

LORD WINDERMERE. And as for your blunder in taking my wife's fan from here, and then leaving it about in Darlington's rooms, it is unpardonable. I can't bear the sight of it now. I shall never let my wife use it again. The thing is soiled for me. You should have kept it, and not brought it back.

MRS. ERLYNNE. I think I *shall* keep it. (*Goes up.*) It's extremely pretty. (*Takes up fan.*) I shall ask Margaret to give it to me.

LORD WINDERMERE. I hope my wife will give it to you.

MRS. ERLYNNE. Oh, I'm sure she will have no objection.

LORD WINDERMERE. I wish that at the same time she would give you a miniature she kisses every night before she prays—it's the miniature of a young, innocent-looking girl with beautiful dark hair.

MRS. ERLYNNE. Ah, yes, I remember. How long ago that seems! (*Goes to sofa and sits down.*) It was done before I was married. Dark hair and an innocent expression were the fashion then, Windermere! (*A pause.*)

LORD WINDERMERE. What do you mean by coming here this morning? What is your object? (*Crossing L. C. and sitting.*)

MRS. ERLYNNE (*with a note of irony in her voice*). To bid good-bye to my dear daughter, of course. (LORD WINDERMERE *bites his underlip in anger.* MRS. ERLYNNE *looks at him, and her voice and manner become serious. In her accents as she talks there is a note of deep tragedy. For a moment she reveals herself.*) Oh, don't imagine I am going to have a pathetic scene with her, weep on her neck and tell her who I am, and all that kind of thing. I have no ambition to play the part of a mother. Only once in my life have I known a mother's feelings. That was last night. They were terrible—they made me suffer—they made me suffer too much. For twenty years, as you say, I have lived childless—I want to live childless still. (*Hiding her feelings with a trivial laugh.*) Besides, my dear Windermere, how on earth could I pose as a mother with a grown-up daughter? Margaret is twenty-one, and I have never admitted that I am more than twenty-nine, or thirty, at the most. Twenty-nine when there are pink shades, thirty when there are not. So you see what difficulties it would involve. No, as far as I am concerned, let your wife cherish the memory of this dead, stainless mother. Why should I interfere with her illusions? I find it hard enough to keep my own. I lost one illusion last night. I thought I had no heart. I find I have, and a heart doesn't suit me, Windermere. Somehow it doesn't go with modern dress. It makes one look old. (*Takes up hand-mirror from table and looks into it.*) And it spoils one's career at critical moments.

LORD WINDERMERE. You fill me with horror—with absolute horror.

MRS. ERLYNNE (*rising*). I suppose, Windermere, you would like me to retire into a convent or become a hospital nurse or something of that kind, as people do in silly modern novels. That is stupid of you, Arthur; in real life we don't do such things—not as long as we have any good looks left, at any rate. No—what consoles one now-a-days is not repentance, but pleasure. Repentance is quite out of date. And besides, if a woman really repents, she has to go to a bad dressmaker, otherwise no one believes in her. And nothing in the world would induce me to do that. No, I am going to pass entirely out of your two lives. My coming into them has been a mistake—I discovered that last night.

LORD WINDERMERE. A fatal mistake.

MRS. ERLYNNE (*smiling*). Almost fatal.

LORD WINDERMERE. I am sorry now I did not tell my wife the whole thing at once.

MRS. ERLYNNE. I regret my bad actions. You regret your good ones—that is the difference between us.

LORD WINDERMERE. I don't trust you. I *will* tell my wife. It's better for her to know, and from me. It will cause her infinite pain—it will humiliate her terribly, but it's right that she should know.

MRS. ERLYNNE. You propose to tell her?

LORD WINDERMERE. I am going to tell her.

MRS. ERLYNNE (*going up to him*). If you do, I will make my name so infamous that it will mar every moment of her life. It will ruin her and make her wretched. If you dare to tell her, there is no depth of degradation I will not sink to, no pit of shame I will not enter. You shall not tell her—I forbid you.

LORD WINDERMERE. Why?

MRS. ERLYNNE (*after a pause*). If I said to you that I cared for her, perhaps loved her even—you would sneer at me, wouldn't you?

LORD WINDERMERE. I should feel it was not true. A mother's love means devotion, unselfishness, sacrifice. What could you know of such things?

MRS. ERLYNNE. You are right. What could I know of such things? Don't let us talk any more about it. As for telling my daughter who I am, that I do not allow. It is my secret, it is not yours. If I make up my mind to tell her, and I think I will, I shall tell her before I leave this house—if not, I shall never tell her.

LORD WINDERMERE (*angrily*). Then let me beg of you to leave our house at once. I will make your excuses to Margaret.

(*Enter* LADY WINDERMERE R. *She goes over to* MRS. ERLYNNE *with the photograph in her hand.* LORD WINDERMERE *moves to back of sofa, and anxiously watches* MRS. ERLYNNE *as the scene progresses.*)

LADY WINDERMERE. I am so sorry, Mrs. Erlynne, to have kept you waiting. I couldn't find the photograph anywhere. At last I discovered it in my husband's dressing-room—he had stolen it.

MRS. ERLYNNE (*takes photograph from her and looks at it*). I am not surprised—it is charming. (*Goes over to sofa with* LADY WINDERMERE *and sits down beside her. Looks again at the photograph.*) And so that is your little boy! What is he called?

LADY WINDERMERE. Gerald, after my dear father.

MRS. ERLYNNE (*laying the photograph down*). Really?

LADY WINDERMERE. Yes. If it had been a girl, I would have called it after my mother. My mother had the same name as myself, Margaret.

MRS. ERLYNNE. My name is Margaret, too.

LADY WINDERMERE. Indeed!

MRS. ERLYNNE. Yes. (*Pause.*) You are devoted to your mother's memory, Lady Windermere, your husband tells me.

LADY WINDERMERE. We all have ideals in life. At least we all should have. Mine is my mother.

MRS. ERLYNNE. Ideals are dangerous things. Realities are better. They wound, but they are better.

LADY WINDERMERE (*shaking her head*). If I lost my ideals, I should lose everything.

MRS. ERLYNNE. Everything?

LADY WINDERMERE. Yes. (*Pause.*)

MRS. ERLYNNE. Did your father often speak to you of your mother?

LADY WINDERMERE. No, it gave him too much pain. He told me how my mother had died a few months after I was born. His eyes filled with tears as he spoke. Then he begged me never to mention her name to him again. It made him suffer even to hear it. My father—my father really died of a broken heart. His was the most ruined life I know.

MRS. ERLYNNE (*rising*). I am afraid I must go now, Lady Windermere.

LADY WINDERMERE (*rising*). Oh, no, don't.

MRS. ERLYNNE. I think I had better. My carriage must have come back by this time. I sent it to Lady Jedburgh's with a note.

LADY WINDERMERE. Arthur, would you mind seeing if Mrs. Erlynne's carriage has come back?

MRS. ERLYNNE. Pray don't trouble Lord Windermere, Lady Windermere.

LADY WINDERMERE. Yes, Arthur, do go, please. (LORD WINDERMERE *hesitates for a moment and looks at* MRS. ERLYNNE. *She remains quite impassive. He leaves the room. To* MRS. ERLYNNE.) Oh! What am I to say to you? You saved me last night! (*Goes towards her.*)

MRS. ERLYNNE. Hush—don't speak of it.

LADY WINDERMERE. I must speak of it. I can't let you think that I am going to accept this sacrifice. I am not. It is too great. I am going to tell my husband everything. It is my duty.

MRS. ERLYNNE. It is not your duty—at least you have duties to others besides him. You say you owe me something?

LADY WINDERMERE. I owe you everything.

MRS. ERLYNNE. Then pay your debt by silence. That is the only way in which it can be paid. Don't spoil the one good thing I have done in my life by telling it to anyone. Promise me that what passed last night will remain a secret between us. You must not bring misery into your husband's life. Why spoil his love? You must not spoil it. Love is easily killed. Oh, how easily love is killed! Pledge me your word, Lady Windermere, that you will *never* tell him. I insist upon it.

LADY WINDERMERE (*with bowed head*). It is your will, not mine.

MRS. ERLYNNE. Yes, it is my will. And never forget your child—I like to think of you as a mother. I like you to think of yourself as one.

LADY WINDERMERE (*looking up*). I always will now. Only once in my life I have forgotten my own mother—

that was last night. Oh, if I had remembered her, I should not have been so foolish, so wicked.

MRS. ERLYNNE (*with a slight shudder*). Hush, last night is quite over.

(*Enter* LORD WINDERMERE.)

LORD WINDERMERE. Your carriage has not come back yet, Mrs. Erlynne.

MRS. ERLYNNE. It makes no matter. I'll take a hansom. There is nothing in the world so respectable as a good Shrewsbury and Talbot. And now, dear Lady Windermere, I am afraid it is really good-bye. (*Moves* UP C.) Oh, I remember. You'll think me absurd, but do you know, I've taken a great fancy to this fan that I was silly enough to run away with last night from your ball. Now I wonder, would you give it to me? Lord Windermere says you may. I know it is his present.

LADY WINDERMERE. Oh, certainly, if it will give you any pleasure. But it has my name on it. It has "Margaret" on it.

MRS. ERLYNNE. But we have the same Christian name.

LADY WINDERMERE. Oh, I forgot. Of course, do have it. What a wonderful chance our names being the same!

MRS. ERLYNNE. Quite wonderful. Thanks—it will always remind me of you. (*Shakes hands with her.*)

(*Enter* PARKER.)

PARKER. Lord Augustus Lorton. Mrs. Erlynne's carriage has come.

(*Enter* LORD AUGUSTUS.)

LORD AUGUSTUS. Good-morning, dear boy. Good-morning, Lady Windermere. (*Sees* MRS. ERLYNNE.) Mrs. Erlynne!

MRS. ERLYNNE. How do you do, Lord Augustus? Are you quite well this morning?

LORD AUGUSTUS (*coldly*). Quite well, thank you, Mrs. Erlynne.

MRS. ERLYNNE. You don't look at all well, Lord Augustus. You stop up too late—it is so bad for you. You really should take more care of yourself. Good-bye, Lord Windermere. (*Goes towards door with a bow to* LORD AUGUSTUS. *Suddenly smiles, and looks back at him.*) Lord Augustus! Won't you see me to my carriage? You might carry the fan.

LORD WINDERMERE. Allow me!

MRS. ERLYNNE. No, I want Lord Augustus. I have a special message for the dear Duchess. Won't you carry the fan, Lord Augustus?

LORD AUGUSTUS. If you really desire it, Mrs. Erlynne.

MRS. ERLYNNE (*laughing*). Of course I do. You'll carry it so gracefully. You would carry off anything gracefully, dear Lord Augustus. (*When she reaches the door she looks back for a moment at* LADY WINDERMERE. *Their eyes meet. Then she turns, and exits* C., followed by LORD AUGUSTUS.)

LADY WINDERMERE. You will never speak against Mrs. Erlynne again, Arthur, will you?

LORD WINDERMERE (*gravely*). She is better than one thought her.

LADY WINDERMERE. She is better than I am.

LORD WINDERMERE (*smiling as he strokes her hair*). Child, you and she belong to different worlds. Into your world evil has never entered.

LADY WINDERMERE. Don't say that, Arthur. There is the same world for all of us, and good and evil, sin and innocence, go through it hand in hand. To shut one's eyes to half of life that one may live securely is as though one blinded oneself that one might walk with more safety in a land of pit and precipice.

LORD WINDERMERE (*moves* DOWN *with her*). Darling, why do you say that?

LADY WINDERMERE (*sits on sofa*). Because I, who had shut my eyes to life, came to the brink. And one who had separated us—

LORD WINDERMERE. We were never parted.

LADY WINDERMERE. We never must be again. Oh, Arthur, don't love me less, and I will trust you more. I will trust you absolutely. Let us go to Selby. In the Rose Garden at Selby, the roses are white and red.

(*Enter* LORD AUGUSTUS c.)

LORD AUGUSTUS. Arthur, she has explained everything! (LADY WINDERMERE *looks horribly frightened.* LORD WINDERMERE *starts.* LORD AUGUSTUS *takes* LORD WINDERMERE *by the arm, and brings him to front of stage.*) My dear fellow, she has explained every demmed thing. We all wronged her immensely. It was entirely for my sake she went to Darlington's rooms—called first at the club. Fact is, wanted to put me out of suspense, and being told I had gone on, followed—naturally—frightened when she heard a lot of men coming in—retired to another room—I assure you, most gratifying to me, the whole thing. We all behaved brutally to her. She is just the woman for me. Suits me down to the ground. All the condition she makes is that we live out of England—a very good thing, too!—Demmed clubs, demmed climate, demmed cooks, demmed everything! Sick of it all.

LADY WINDERMERE (*frightened*). Has Mrs. Erlynne—

LORD AUGUSTUS (*advancing towards her with a bow*). Yes, Lady Windermere, Mrs. Erlynne has done me the honor of accepting my hand.

LORD WINDERMERE. Well, you are certainly marrying a very clever woman.

LADY WINDERMERE (*taking her husband's hand*). Ah! you're marrying a very good woman.

CURTAIN

The Importance of Being Earnest

A Trivial Comedy
for
Serious People

ह৯

CHARACTERS

JOHN WORTHING, J.P.	LANE (*Manservant*)
ALGERNON MONCRIEFF	LADY BRACKNELL
REV. CANON CHASUBLE, D. D.	HON. GWENDOLEN FAIRFAX
	CECILY CARDEW
MERRIMAN (*Butler*)	MISS PRISM (*Governess*)

THE SCENES OF THE PLAY

ACT I. Algernon Moncrieff's Flat in Half-Moon Street, W.

ACT II. The Garden at the Manor House, Woolton.

ACT III. Drawing-room of the Manor House, Woolton.

TIME. — The Present. PLACE. — London.

ACT I

SCENE.—*Morning-room in* ALGERNON'S *flat in Half-Moon Street. The room is luxuriously and artistically furnished. The sound of a piano is heard in the adjoining room. (*LANE *is arranging afternoon tea on the table, and after the music has ceased,* ALGERNON *enters.*)*

ALGERNON. Did you hear what I was playing, Lane?

LANE. I didn't think it polite to listen, sir.

ALGERNON. I'm sorry for that, for your sake. I don't play accurately—anyone can play accurately—but I play with wonderful expression. As far as the piano is concerned, sentiment is my forte. I keep science for Life.

LANE. Yes, sir.

ALGERNON. And, speaking of the science of Life, have you got the cucumber sandwiches cut for Lady Bracknell?

LANE. Yes, sir. (*Hands them on a salver.*)

ALGERNON (*inspects them, takes two, and sits down on the sofa*). Oh! . . . by the way, Lane, I see from your book that on Thursday night, when Lord Shoreman and Mr. Worthing were dining with me, eight bottles of champagne are entered as having been consumed.

LANE. Yes, sir; eight bottles and a pint.

ALGERNON. Why is it that at a bachelor's establishment the servants invariably drink the champagne? I ask merely for information.

LANE. I attribute it to the superior quality of the wine, sir. I have often observed that in married households the champagne is rarely of a first-rate brand.

ALGERNON. Good heavens! Is marriage so demoralizing as that?

LANE. I believe it *is* a very pleasant state, sir. I have had very little experience of it myself up to the present. I have only been married once. That was in consequence of a misunderstanding between myself and a young woman.

ALGERNON (*languidly*). I don't know that I am much interested in your family life, Lane.

LANE. No, sir; it is not a very interesting subject. I never think of it myself.

ALGERNON. Very natural, I am sure. That will do, Lane, thank you.

LANE. Thank you, sir. (*Goes out.*)

ALGERNON. Lane's views on marriage seem somewhat lax. Really, if the lower orders don't set us a good example, what on earth is the use of them? They seem, as a class, to have absolutely no sense of moral responsibility.

(*Enter* LANE.)

LANE. Mr. Ernest Worthing.

(*Enter* JACK. LANE *goes out.*)

ALGERNON. How are you, my dear Ernest? What brings you up to town?

JACK. Oh, pleasure, pleasure! What else should bring one anywhere? Eating as usual, I see, Algy!

ALGERNON (*stiffly*). I believe it is customary in good society to take some slight refreshment at five o'clock. Where have you been since last Thursday?

JACK (*sitting down on the sofa*). In the country.

ALGERNON. What on earth do you do there?

JACK (*pulling off his gloves*). When one is in town one amuses oneself. When one is in the country one amuses other people. It is excessively boring.

ALGERNON. And who are the people you amuse?

JACK (*airily*). Oh, neighbours, neighbours.

ALGERNON. Got nice neighbours in your part of Shropshire?

JACK. Perfectly horrid! Never speak to one of them.

ALGERNON. How immensely you must amuse them! (*Goes over and takes sandwich.*) By the way, Shropshire is your county, is it not?

JACK. Eh? Shropshire? Yes, of course. Hallo! Why all these cups? Why cucumber sandwiches? Why such reckless extravagance in one so young? Who is coming to tea?

ALGERNON. Oh! merely Aunt Augusta and Gwendolen.

JACK. How perfectly delightful!

ALGERNON. Yes, that is all very well; but I am afraid Aunt Augusta won't quite approve of your being here.

JACK. May I ask why?

ALGERNON. My dear fellow, the way you flirt with Gwendolen is perfectly disgraceful. It is almost as bad as the way Gwendolen flirts with you.

JACK. I am in love with Gwendolen. I have come up to town expressly to propose to her.

ALGERNON. I thought you had come up for pleasure? . . . I call that business.

JACK. How utterly unromantic you are!

ALGERNON. I really don't see anything romantic in proposing. It is very romantic to be in love. But there is nothing romantic about a definite proposal. Why, one may be accepted. One usually is, I believe. Then the excitement is all over. The very essence of romance is uncertainty. If ever I get married, I'll certainly try to forget the fact.

JACK. I have no doubt about that, dear Algy. The Divorce Court was specially invented for people whose memories are so curiously constituted.

ALGERNON. Oh! there is no use speculating on that subject. Divorces are made in Heaven——(JACK *puts out his hand to take a sandwich.* ALGERNON *at once interferes.*) Please don't touch the cucumber sandwiches. They are ordered specially for Aunt Augusta. (*Takes one and eats it.*)

JACK. Well, you have been eating them all the time.

ALGERNON. That is quite a different matter. She is my aunt. (*Takes plate from below.*) Have some bread and butter. The bread and butter is for Gwendolen. Gwendolen is devoted to bread and butter.

JACK (*advancing to table and helping himself*). And very good bread and butter it is, too.

ALGERNON. Well, my dear fellow, you need not eat as if you were going to eat it all. You behave as if you were married to her already. You are not married to her already, and I don't think you ever will be.

JACK. Why on earth do you say that?

ALGERNON. Well, in the first place girls never marry the men they flirt with. Girls don't think it right.

JACK. Oh, that is nonsense!

ALGERNON. It isn't. It is a great truth. It accounts for the extraordinary number of bachelors that one sees all over the place. In the second place, I don't give my consent.

JACK. Your consent!

ALGERNON. My dear fellow, Gwendolen is my first cousin. And before I allow you to marry her, you will have to clear up the whole question of Cecily. (*Rings bell.*)

JACK. Cecily! What on earth do you mean? What do you mean, Algy, by Cecily? I don't know anyone of the name of Cecily.

(*Enter* LANE.)

ALGERNON. Bring me that cigarette case Mr. Worthing left in the smoking-room the last time he dined here.

LANE. Yes, sir. (*Goes out.*)

JACK. Do you mean to say you have had my cigarette case all this time? I wish to goodness you had let me know. I have been writing frantic letters to Scotland Yard about it. I was very nearly offering a large reward.

ALGERNON. Well, I wish you would offer one. I happen to be more than usually hard up.

JACK. There is no good offering a large reward now that the thing is found.

(*Enter* LANE *with the cigarette case on a salver.* ALGERNON *takes it at once.* LANE *goes out.*)

ALGERNON. I think that is rather mean of you, Ernest, I must say. (*Opens case and examines it.*) However, it makes no matter, for, now that I look at the inscription, I find that the thing isn't yours after all.

JACK. Of course it's mine. (*Moving to him.*) You have seen me with it a hundred times, and you have no right whatsoever to read what is written inside. It is a very ungentlemanly thing to read a private cigarette case.

ALGERNON. Oh! it is absurd to have a hard-and-fast rule about what one should read and what one shouldn't. More than half of modern culture depends on what one shouldn't read.

JACK. I am quite aware of the fact, and I don't propose to discuss modern culture. It isn't the sort of thing one should talk of in private. I simply want my cigarette case back.

ALGERNON. Yes; but this isn't your cigarette case. This cigarette case is a present from someone of the name of Cecily, and you said you didn't know anyone of that name.

JACK. Well, if you want to know, Cecily happens to be my aunt.

ALGERNON. Your aunt!

JACK. Yes. Charming old lady she is, too. Lives at Tunbridge Wells. Just give it back to me, Algy.

ALGERNON (*retreating to back of sofa*). But why does she call herself little Cecily if she is your aunt and lives at Tunbridge Wells? (*Reading.*) "From little Cecily with her fondest love."

JACK (*moving to sofa and kneeling upon it*). My dear fellow, what on earth is there in that? Some aunts are tall, some aunts are not tall. That is a matter that surely an aunt may be allowed to decide for herself. You seem to think that every aunt should be exactly like your aunt! That is absurd! For heaven's sake give me back my cigarette case. (*Follows* ALGERNON *round the room.*)

ALGERNON. Yes. But why does your aunt call you her uncle? "From little Cecily, with her fondest love to her dear Uncle Jack." There is no objection, I admit, to an aunt being a small aunt, but why an aunt, no matter what her size may be, should call her own nephew her uncle, I can't quite make out. Besides, your name isn't Jack at all; it is Ernest.

JACK. It isn't Ernest; it's Jack.

ALGERNON. You have always told me it was Ernest. I have introduced you to everyone as Ernest. You answer to the name of Ernest. You look as if your name was Ernest. You are the most earnest looking person I ever saw in my life. It is perfectly absurd your saying that your name isn't Ernest. It's on your cards. Here is one of them. (*Taking it from case.*) "Mr. Ernest Worthing, B 4, The Albany." I'll keep this as a proof your name is Ernest if ever you attempt to deny it to me, or to Gwendolen, or to anyone else. (*Puts the card in his pocket.*)

JACK. Well, my name is Ernest in town and Jack in the country, and the cigarette case was given to me in the country.

ALGERNON. Yes, but that does not account for the fact that your small Aunt Cecily, who lives at Tunbridge

Wells, calls you her dear uncle. Come, old boy, you had much better have the thing out at once.

JACK. My dear Algy, you talk exactly as if you were a dentist. It is very vulgar to talk like a dentist when one isn't a dentist. It produces a false impression.

ALGERNON. Well, that is exactly what dentists always do. Now, go on! Tell me the whole thing. I may mention that I have always suspected you of being a confirmed and secret Bunburyist; and I am quite sure of it now.

JACK. Bunburyist? What on earth do you mean by a Bunburyist?

ALGERNON. I'll reveal to you the meaning of that incomparable expression as soon as you are kind enough to inform me why you are Ernest in town and Jack in the country.

JACK. Well, produce my cigarette case first.

ALGERNON. Here it is. (*Hands cigarette case.*) Now produce your explanation, and pray make it improbable. (*Sits on sofa.*)

JACK. My dear fellow, there is nothing improbable about my explanation at all. In fact it's perfectly ordinary. Old Mr. Thomas Cardew, who adopted me when I was a little boy, made me in his will guardian to his granddaughter, Miss Cecily Cardew. Cecily, who addresses me as her uncle from motives of respect that you could not possibly appreciate, lives at my place in the country under the charge of her admirable governess, Miss Prism.

ALGERNON. Where is that place in the country, by the way?

JACK. That is nothing to you, dear boy. You are not going to be invited. . . . I may tell you candidly that the place is not in Shropshire.

ALGERNON. I suspected that, my dear fellow! I have Bunburyed all over Shropshire on two separate occasions. Now, go on. Why are you Ernest in town and Jack in the country?

JACK. My dear Algy, I don't know whether you will be able to understand my real motives. You are hardly serious enough. When one is placed in the position of guardian, one has to adopt a very high moral tone on all subjects. It's one's duty to do so. And as a high moral tone can hardly be said to conduce very much to either one's health or one's happiness, in order to get up to town I have always pretended to have a younger brother of the name of Ernest, who lives in the Albany, and gets into the most dreadful scrapes. That, my dear Algy, is the whole truth pure and simple.

ALGERNON. The truth is rarely pure and never simple. Modern life would be very tedious if it were either, and modern literature a complete impossibility!

JACK. That wouldn't be at all a bad thing.

ALGERNON. Literary criticism is not your forte, my dear fellow. Don't try it. You should leave that to people who haven't been at a University. They do it so well in the daily papers. What you really are is a Bunburyist. I was quite right in saying you were a Bunburyist. You are one of the most advanced Bunburyists I know.

JACK. What on earth do you mean?

ALGERNON. You have invented a very useful younger brother called Ernest, in order that you may be able to come up to town as often as you like. I have invented an invaluable permanent invalid called Bunbury, in order that I may be able to go down into the country whenever I choose. Bunbury is perfectly invaluable. If it wasn't for Bunbury's extraordinary bad health, for instance, I wouldn't be able to dine with you at Willis's to-night, for I have been really engaged to Aunt Augusta for more than a week.

JACK. I haven't asked you to dine with me anywhere tonight.

ALGERNON. I know. You are absolutely careless about sending out invitations. It is very foolish of you. Nothing annoys people so much as not receiving invitations.

JACK. You had much better dine with your Aunt Augusta.

ALGERNON. I haven't the smallest intention of doing anything of the kind. To begin with, I dined there on Monday, and once a week is quite enough to dine with one's own relatives. In the second place, whenever I do dine there I am always treated as a member of the family, and sent down with either no woman at all, or two. In the third place, I know perfectly well whom she will place me next to, to-night. She will place me next Mary Farquhar, who always flirts with her own husband across the dinner-table. That is not very pleasant. Indeed, it is not even decent . . . and that sort of thing is enormously on the increase. The amount of women in London who flirt with their own husbands is perfectly scandalous. It looks so bad. It is simply washing one's clean linen in public. Besides, now that I know you to be a confirmed Bunburyist I naturally want to talk to you about Bunburying. I want to tell you the rules.

JACK. I'm not a Bunburyist at all. If Gwendolen accepts me, I am going to kill my brother; indeed I think I'll kill him in any case. Cecily is a little too much interested in him. It is rather a bore. So I am going to get rid of Ernest. And I strongly advise you to do the same with Mr. . . . with your invalid friend who has the absurd name.

ALGERNON. Nothing will induce me to part with Bunbury, and if you ever get married, which seems to me extremely problematic, you will be very glad to know Bunbury. A man who marries without knowing Bunbury has a very tedious time of it.

JACK. That is nonsense. If I marry a charming girl like Gwendolen, and she is the only girl I ever saw in my life that I would marry, I certainly won't want to know Bunbury.

ALGERNON. Then your wife will. You don't seem to

realize that in married life three is company and two is none.

JACK (*sententiously*). That, my dear young friend, is the theory that the corrupt French Drama has been propounding for the last fifty years.

ALGERNON. Yes; and that the happy English home has proved in half the time.

JACK. For heaven's sake, don't try to be cynical. It's perfectly easy to be cynical.

ALGERNON. My dear fellow, it isn't easy to be anything now-a-days. There's such a lot of beastly competition about. (*The sound of an electric bell is heard.*) Ah! that must be Aunt Augusta. Only relatives, or creditors, ever ring in that Wagnerian manner. Now, if I get her out of the way for ten minutes, so that you can have an opportunity for proposing to Gwendolen, may I dine with you to-night at Willis's?

JACK. I suppose so if you want to.

ALGERNON. Yes, but you must be serious about it. I hate people who are not serious about meals. It is so shallow of them.

(*Enter* LANE.)

LANE. Lady Bracknell and Miss Fairfax. (ALGERNON *goes forward to meet them. Enter* LADY BRACKNELL *and* GWENDOLEN.)

LADY BRACKNELL. Good afternoon, dear Algernon, I hope you are behaving very well.

ALGERNON. I'm feeling very well, Aunt Augusta.

LADY BRACKNELL. That's not quite the same thing. In fact the two things rarely go together. (*Sees* JACK *and bows to him with icy coldness.*)

ALGERNON (*to* GWENDOLEN). Dear me, you are smart!

GWENDOLEN. I am always smart! Aren't I, Mr. Worthing?

JACK. You're quite perfect, Miss Fairfax.

GWENDOLEN. Oh! I hope I am not that. It would leave no room for developments, and I intend to develop in *many directions.* (GWENDOLEN *and* JACK *sit down together in the corner.*)

LADY BRACKNELL. I'm sorry if we are a little late, Algernon, but I was obliged to call on dear Lady Harbury. I hadn't been there since her poor husband's death. I never saw a woman so altered; she looks quite twenty years younger. And now I'll have a cup of tea, and one of those nice cucumber sandwiches you promised me.

ALGERNON. Certainly, Aunt Augusta. (*Goes over to tea-table.*)

LADY BRACKNELL. Won't you come and sit here, Gwendolen?

GWENDOLEN. Thanks, Mamma. I'm quite comfortable where I am.

ALGERNON (*picking up empty plate in horror*). Good heavens! Lane! Why are there no cucumber sandwiches? I ordered them specially.

LANE (*gravely*). There were no cucumbers in the market this morning, sir. I went down twice.

ALGERNON. No cucumbers!

LANE. No, sir. Not even for ready money.

ALGERNON. That will do, Lane, thank you.

LANE. Thank you, sir. (*Goes out.*)

ALGERNON. I am greatly distressed, Aunt Augusta, about there being no cucumbers, not even for ready money.

LADY BRACKNELL. It really makes no matter, Algernon. I had some crumpets with Lady Harbury, who seems to me to be living entirely for pleasure now.

ALGERNON. I hear her hair has turned quite gold from grief.

LADY BRACKNELL. It certainly has changed its colour. From what cause I, of course, cannot say. (ALGERNON *crosses and hands tea.*) Thank you. I've quite a treat for you to-night, Algernon. I am going to send you down with Mary Farquhar. She is such a nice woman, and so attentive to her husband. It's delightful to watch them.

ALGERNON. I am afraid, Aunt Augusta, I shall have to give up the pleasure of dining with you to-night after all.

LADY BRACKNELL (*frowning*). I hope not, Algernon. It would put my table completely out. Your uncle would have to dine upstairs. Fortunately he is accustomed to that.

ALGERNON. It is a great bore, and, I need hardly say, a terrible disappointment to me, but the fact is I have just had a telegram to say that my poor friend Bunbury is very ill again. (*Exchanges glances with* JACK.) They seem to think I should be with him.

LADY BRACKNELL. It is very strange. This Mr. Bunbury seems to suffer from curiously bad health.

ALGERNON. Yes; poor Bunbury is a dreadful invalid.

LADY BRACKNELL. Well, I must say, Algernon, that I think it is high time that Mr. Bunbury made up his mind whether he was going to live or to die. This shilly-shallying with the question is absurd. Nor do I in any way approve of the modern sympathy with invalids. I consider it morbid. Illness of any kind is hardly a thing to be encouraged in others. Health is the primary duty of life. I am always telling that to your poor uncle, but he never seems to take much notice . . . as far as any improvement in his ailments goes. I should be much obliged if you would ask Mr. Bunbury, from me, to be kind enough not to have a relapse on Saturday, for I rely on you to arrange my music for me. It is my last reception and one wants something that will encourage conversation, particularly at the end of the season when everyone has practically said whatever they had to say, which, in most cases, was probably not much.

ALGERNON. I'll speak to Bunbury, Aunt Augusta, if he is still conscious, and I think I can promise you he'll be all right by Saturday. You see, if one plays good music, people don't listen, and if one plays bad music people don't talk. But I'll run over the programme I've drawn out, if you will kindly come into the next room for a moment.

LADY BRACKNELL. Thank you, Algernon. It is very thoughtful of you. (*Rising, and following* ALGERNON.) I'm sure the programme will be delightful, after a few expurgations. French songs I cannot possibly allow. People always seem to think that they are improper, and either look shocked, which is vulgar, or laugh, which is worse. But German sounds a thoroughly respectable language, and indeed, I believe is so. Gwendolen, you will accompany me.

GWENDOLEN. Certainly, Mamma. (LADY BRACKNELL *and* ALGERNON *go into the music-room;* GWENDOLEN *remains behind.*)

JACK. Charming day it has been, Miss Fairfax.

GWENDOLEN. Pray don't talk to me about the weather, Mr. Worthing. Whenever people talk to me about the weather, I always feel quite certain that they mean something else. And that makes me so nervous.

JACK. I do mean something else.

GWENDOLEN. I thought so. In fact, I am never wrong.

JACK. And I would like to be allowed to take advantage of Lady Bracknell's temporary absence . . .

GWENDOLEN. I would certainly advise you to do so. Mamma has a way of coming back suddenly into a room that I have often had to speak to her about.

JACK (*nervously*). Miss Fairfax, ever since I met you I have admired you more than any girl . . . I have ever met since . . . I met you.

GWENDOLEN. Yes, I am quite aware of the fact. And I often wish that in public, at any rate, you had been more demonstrative. For me you have always had an irresistible fascination. Even before I met you I was far from indifferent to you. (JACK *looks at her in amazement.*) We live, as I hope you know, Mr. Worthing, in an age of ideals. The fact is constantly mentioned in the more expensive monthly magazines, and has reached the provincial pulpits, I am told: and my ideal has always been to love some one of the name of Ernest. There is something in that name that inspires absolute confidence. The moment Algernon first mentioned to me that he had a friend called Ernest, I knew I was destined to love you.

JACK. You really love me, Gwendolen?

GWENDOLEN. Passionately!

JACK. Darling! You don't know how happy you've made me.

GWENDOLEN. My own Ernest!

JACK. But you don't really mean to say that you couldn't love me if my name wasn't Ernest?

GWENDOLEN. But your name is Ernest.

JACK. Yes, I know it is. But supposing it was something else? Do you mean to say you couldn't love me then?

GWENDOLEN (*glibly*). Ah! that is clearly a metaphysical speculation, and like most metaphysical speculations has very little reference at all to the actual facts of real life, as we know them.

JACK. Personally, darling, to speak quite candidly, I don't much care about the name of Ernest. . . . I don't think that name suits me at all.

GWENDOLEN. It suits you perfectly. It is a divine name. It has a music of its own. It produces vibrations.

JACK. Well, really, Gwendolen, I must say that I think there are lots of other much nicer names. I think Jack, for instance, a charming name.

GWENDOLEN. Jack? . . . No, there is very little music in the name Jack, if any at all, indeed. It does not thrill. It produces absolutely no vibration. . . . I have known several Jacks, and they all, without exception, were more than usually plain. Besides, Jack is a notorious domesticity for John! And I pity any woman who is married to a man called John. She would probably never be allowed to know the entrancing pleasure of a single moment's solitude. The only really safe name is Ernest.

JACK. Gwendolen, I must get christened at once—I mean we must get married at once. There is no time to be lost.

GWENDOLEN. Married, Mr. Worthing?

JACK (*astounded*). Well ... surely. You know that I love you, and you led me to believe, Miss Fairfax, that you were not absolutely indifferent to me.

GWENDOLEN. I adore you. But you haven't proposed to me yet. Nothing has been said at all about marriage. The subject has not even been touched on.

JACK. Well ... may I propose to you now?

GWENDOLEN. I think it would be an admirable opportunity. And to spare you any possible disappointment, Mr. Worthing, I think it only fair to tell you quite frankly beforehand that I am fully determined to accept you.

JACK. Gwendolen!

GWENDOLEN. Yes, Mr. Worthing, what have you got to say to me?

JACK. You know what I have got to say to you.

GWENDOLEN. Yes, but you don't say it.

JACK. Gwendolen, will you marry me? (*Goes on his knees.*)

GWENDOLEN. Of course I will, darling. How long you have been about it! I am afraid you have had very little experience in how to propose.

JACK. My own one, I have never loved anyone in the world but you.

GWENDOLEN. Yes, but men often propose for practice. I know my brother Gerald does. All my girl-friends tell me so. What wonderfully blue eyes you have, Ernest! They are quite, quite blue. I hope you will always look at me just like that, especially when there are other people present.

(*Enter* LADY BRACKNELL.)

LADY BRACKNELL. Mr. Worthing! Rise, sir, from this semi-recumbent posture. It is most indecorous.

GWENDOLEN. Mamma! (*He tried to rise; she restrains him.*) I must beg you to retire. This is no place for you. Besides, Mr. Worthing has not quite finished yet.

LADY BRACKNELL. Finished what, may I ask?

GWENDOLEN. I am engaged to Mr. Worthing, Mamma. (*They rise together.*)

LADY BRACKNELL. Pardon me, you are not engaged to anyone. When you do become engaged to some one, I, or your father, should his health permit him, will inform you of the fact. An engagement should come on a young girl as a surprise, pleasant or unpleasant, as the case may be. It is hardly a matter that she could be allowed to arrange for herself. . . . And now I have a few questions to put to you, Mr. Worthing. While I am making these inquiries, you, Gwendolen, will wait for me below in the carriage.

GWENDOLEN (*reproachfully*). Mamma!

LADY BRACKNELL. In the carriage, Gwendolen! (GWENDOLEN *goes to the door. She and* JACK *blow kisses to each other behind* LADY BRACKNELL's *back.* LADY BRACKNELL *looks vaguely about as if she could not understand what the noise was. Finally turns round.*) Gwendolen, the carriage!

GWENDOLEN. Yes, Mamma. (*Goes out, looking back at* JACK.)

LADY BRACKNELL (*sitting down*). You can take a seat, Mr. Worthing. (*Looks in her pocket for notebook and pencil.*)

JACK. Thank you, Lady Bracknell, I prefer standing.

LADY BRACKNELL (*pencil and notebook in hand*). I feel bound to tell you that you are not down on my list of eligible young men, although I have the same list as the dear Duchess of Bolton has. We work together, in fact. However, I am quite ready to enter your name, should your answers be what a really affectionate mother requires. Do you smoke?

JACK. Well, yes, I must admit I smoke.

LADY BRACKNELL. I am glad to hear it. A man should always have an occupation of some kind. There are far too many idle men in London as it is. How old are you?

JACK. Twenty-nine.

LADY BRACKNELL. A very good age to be married at. I have always been of opinion that a man who desires to get married should know either everything or nothing. Which do you know?

JACK (*after some hesitation*). I know nothing, Lady Bracknell.

LADY BRACKNELL. I am pleased to hear it. I do not approve of anything that tampers with natural ignorance. Ignorance is like a delicate exotic fruit; touch it and the bloom is gone. The whole theory of modern education is radically unsound. Fortunately in England, at any rate, education produces no effect whatsoever. If it did, it would prove a serious danger to the upper classes, and probably lead to acts of violence in Grosvenor Square. What is your income?

JACK. Between seven and eight thousand a year.

LADY BRACKNELL (*makes a note in her book*). In land, or in investments?

JACK. In investments, chiefly.

LADY BRACKNELL. That is satisfactory. What between the duties expected of one during one's life-time, and the duties exacted from one after one's death, land has ceased to be either a profit or a pleasure. It gives one position, and prevents one from keeping it up. That's all that can be said about land.

JACK. I have a country house with some land, of course, attached to it, about fifteen hundred acres, I believe; but I don't depend on that for my real income. In fact, as far as I can make out, the poachers are the only people who make anything out of it.

LADY BRACKNELL. A country house! How many bedrooms? Well, that point can be cleared up afterwards. You have a town house, I hope? A girl with a simple, unspoiled nature, like Gwendolen, could hardly be expected to reside in the country.

JACK. Well, I own a house in Belgrave Square, but it is let by the year to Lady Bloxham. Of course, I can get it back whenever I like, at six months' notice.

LADY BRACKNELL. Lady Bloxham? I don't know her.

JACK. Oh, she goes about very little. She is a lady considerably advanced in years.

LADY BRACKNELL. Ah, now-a-days that is no guarantee of respectability of character. What number in Belgrave Square?

JACK. 149.

LADY BRACKNELL (*shaking her head*). The unfashionable side. I thought there was something. However, that could easily be altered.

JACK. Do you mean the fashion, or the side?

LADY BRACKNELL (*sternly*). Both, if necessary, I presume. What are your politics?

JACK. Well, I am afraid I really have none. I am a Liberal Unionist.

LADY BRACKNELL. Oh, they count as Tories. They dine with us. Or come in the evening, at any rate. Now to minor matters. Are your parents living?

JACK. I have lost both my parents.

LADY BRACKNELL. Both? . . . That seems like carelessness. Who was your father? He was evidently a man of some wealth. Was he born in what the Radical papers call the purple of commerce, or did he rise from the ranks of the aristocracy?

JACK. I am afraid I really don't know. The fact is, Lady Bracknell, I said I had lost my parents. It would be nearer the truth to say that my parents seem to have lost me . . . I don't actually know who I am by birth. I was . . . well, I was found.

LADY BRACKNELL. Found!

JACK. The late Mr. Thomas Cardew, an old gentleman of a very charitable and kindly disposition, found me, and gave me the name of Worthing, because he happened to have a first-class ticket for Worthing in his pocket at the time. Worthing is a place in Sussex. It is a seaside resort.

LADY BRACKNELL. Where did the charitable gentleman who had a first-class ticket for this seaside resort find you?

JACK (*gravely*). In a hand-bag.

LADY BRACKNELL. A hand-bag?

JACK (*very seriously*). Yes, Lady Bracknell. I was in a hand-bag—a somewhat large, black leather hand-bag, with handles to it—an ordinary hand-bag in fact.

LADY BRACKNELL. In what locality did Mr. James, or Thomas, Cardew come across this ordinary hand-bag?

JACK. In the cloak-room at Victoria Station. It was given to him in mistake for his own.

LADY BRACKNELL. The cloak-room at Victoria Station?

JACK. Yes. The Brighton line.

LADY BRACKNELL. The line is immaterial. Mr. Worthing, I confess I feel somewhat bewildered by what you have just told me. To be born, or at any rate bred, in a hand-bag, whether it had handles or not, seems to me to display a contempt for the ordinary decencies of family life that remind one of the worst excesses of the French Revolution. And I presume you know what that unfortunate movement led to? As for the particular locality in which the hand-bag was found, a cloak-room at a railway station might serve to conceal a social indiscretion—has probably, indeed, been used for the purpose before now—but it could hardly be regarded as an assured basis for a recognized position in good society.

JACK. May I ask you then what you would advise me to do? I need hardly say I would do anything in the world to ensure Gwendolen's happiness.

LADY BRACKNELL. I would strongly advise you, Mr. Worthing, to try and acquire some relations as soon as possible, and to make a definite effort to produce at any rate one parent, of either sex, before the season is quite over.

JACK. Well, I don't see how I could possibly manage to do that. I can produce the hand-bag at any moment. It is in my dressing-room at home. I really think that should satisfy you, Lady Bracknell.

LADY BRACKNELL. Me, sir! What has it to do with me? You can hardly imagine that I and Lord Brack-nell would dream of allowing our only daughter—a girl brought up with the utmost care—to marry into a cloak-room, and form an alliance with a parcel? Good morning, Mr. Worthing! (LADY BRACKNELL *sweeps out in majestic indignation.*)

JACK. Good morning! (ALGERNON, *from the other room, strikes up the Wedding March.* JACK *looks perfectly furious, and goes to the door.*) For goodness' sake don't play that ghastly tune, Algy! How idiotic you are! (*The music stops, and* ALGERNON *enters cheerily.*)

ALGERNON. Didn't it go off all right, old boy? You don't mean to say Gwendolen refused you? I know it is a way she has. She is always refusing people. I think it is most ill-natured of her.

JACK. Oh, Gwendolen is as right as a trivet. As far as she is concerned, we are engaged. Her mother is per-fectly unbearable. Never met such a Gorgon ... I don't really know what a Gorgon is like, but I am quite sure that Lady Bracknell is one. In any case, she is a monster, without being a myth, which is rather unfair. . . . I beg your pardon, Algy, I suppose I shouldn't talk about your own aunt in that way before you.

ALGERNON. My dear boy, I love hearing my relations abused. It is the only thing that makes me put up with them at all. Relations are simply a tedious pack of peo-ple, who haven't got the remotest knowledge of how to live, nor the smallest instinct about when to die.

JACK. Oh, that is nonsense!

ALGERNON. It isn't!

JACK. Well, I won't argue about the matter. You always want to argue about things.

ALGERNON. That is exactly what things were originally made for.

JACK. Upon my word, if I thought that, I'd shoot myself.... (*A pause.*) You don't think there is any chance of Gwendolen becoming like her mother in about a hundred and fifty years, do you, Algy?

ALGERNON. All women become like their mothers. That is their tragedy. No man does. That's his.

JACK. Is that clever?

ALGERNON. It is perfectly phrased! and quite as true as any observation in civilized life should be.

JACK. I am sick to death of cleverness. Everybody is clever now-a-days. You can't go anywhere without meeting clever people. The thing has become an absolute public nuisance. I wish to goodness we had a few fools left.

ALGERNON. We have.

JACK. I should extremely like to meet them. What do they talk about?

ALGERNON. The fools? Oh! about the clever people, of course.

JACK. What fools!

ALGERNON. By the way, did you tell Gwendolen the truth about your being Ernest in town, and Jack in the country?

JACK (*in a very patronising manner*). My dear fellow, the truth isn't quite the sort of thing one tells to a nice, sweet, refined girl. What extraordinary ideas you have about the way to behave to a woman!

ALGERNON. The only way to behave to a woman is to make love to her, if she is pretty, and to someone else if she is plain.

JACK. Oh, that is nonsense.

ALGERNON. What about your brother? What about the profligate Ernest?

JACK. Oh, before the end of the week I shall have got rid of him. I'll say he died in Paris of apoplexy. Lots of people die of apoplexy, quite suddenly, don't they?

ALGERNON. Yes, but it's hereditary, my dear fellow. It's a sort of thing that runs in families. You had much better say a severe chill.

JACK. You are sure a severe chill isn't hereditary, or anything of that kind?

ALGERNON. Of course it isn't!

JACK. Very well, then. My poor brother Ernest is carried off suddenly in Paris, by a severe chill. That gets rid of him.

ALGERNON. But I thought you said that ... Miss Cardew was a little too much interested in your poor brother Ernest? Won't she feel his loss a good deal?

JACK. Oh, that is all right. Cecily is not a silly, romantic girl, I am glad to say. She has got a capital appetite, goes for long walks, and pays no attention at all to her lessons.

ALGERNON. I would rather like to see Cecily.

JACK. I will take very good care you never do. She is excessively pretty, and she is only just eighteen.

ALGERNON. Have you told Gwendolen yet that you have an excessively pretty ward who is only just eighteen?

JACK. Oh! one doesn't blurt these things out to people. Cecily and Gwendolen are perfectly certain to be extremely great friends. I'll bet you anything you like that half an hour after they have met, they will be calling each other sister.

ALGERNON. Women only do that when they have called each other a lot of other things first. Now, my dear boy, if we want to get a good table at Willis's, we really must go and dress. Do you know it is nearly seven?

JACK (*irritably*). Oh! it always is nearly seven.

ALGERNON. Well, I'm hungry.

JACK. I never knew you when you weren't. . . .

ALGERNON. What shall we do after dinner? Go to a theatre?

JACK. Oh, no! I loathe listening.

ALGERNON. Well, let us go to the Club.

JACK. Oh, no! I hate talking.

ALGERNON. Well, we might trot round to the Empire at ten?

JACK. Oh, no! can't bear looking at things. It is so silly.

ALGERNON. Well, what shall we do?

JACK. Nothing!

ALGERNON. It is awfully hard work doing nothing. However, I don't mind hard work where there is no definite object of any kind.

(*Enter* LANE.)

LANE. Miss Fairfax.

(*Enter* GWENDOLEN. LANE *goes out.*)

ALGERNON. Gwendolen, upon my word!

GWENDOLEN. Algy, kindly turn your back. I have something very particular to say to Mr. Worthing.

ALGERNON. Really, Gwendolen, I don't think I can allow this at all.

GWENDOLEN. Algy, you always adopt a strictly immoral attitude towards life. You are not quite old enough to do that. (ALGERNON *retires to the fireplace.*)

JACK. My own darling!

GWENDOLEN. Ernest, we may never be married. From the expression on Mamma's face I fear we never shall. Few parents now-a-days pay any regard to what their children say to them. The old-fashioned respect for the young is fast dying out. Whatever influence I ever had over Mamma, I lost at the age of three. But although she may prevent us from becoming man and wife, and I may marry someone else, and marry often, nothing that she can possibly do can alter my eternal devotion to you.

JACK. Dear Gwendolen.

GWENDOLEN. The story of your romantic origin, as related to me by Mamma, with unpleasing comments, has naturally stirred the deeper fibers of my nature. Your Christian name has an irresistible fascination. The simplicity of your character makes you exquisitely incomprehensible to me. Your town address at the Albany I have. What is your address in the country?

JACK. The Manor House, Woolton, Hertfordshire. (ALGERNON, *who has been carefully listening, smiles to himself, and writes the address on his shirt-cuff. Then picks up the Railway Guide.*)

GWENDOLEN. There is a good postal service, I suppose? It may be necessary to do something desperate. That, of course, will require serious consideration. I will communicate with you daily.

JACK. My own one!

GWENDOLEN. How long do you remain in town?

JACK. Till Monday.

GWENDOLEN. Good! Algy, you may turn round now.

ALGERNON. Thanks, I've turned round already.

GWENDOLEN. You may also ring the bell.

JACK. You will let me see you to your carriage, my own darling?

GWENDOLEN. Certainly.

JACK (*to* LANE, *who now enters*). I will see Miss Fairfax out.

LANE. Yes, sir. (JACK *and* GWENDOLEN *go off.* LANE *presents several letters on a salver to* ALGERNON. *It is to be surmised that they are bills, as* ALGERNON, *after looking at the envelopes, tears them up.*)

ALGERNON. A glass of sherry, Lane.

LANE. Yes, sir.

ALGERNON. To-morrow, Lane, I'm going Bunburying.

LANE. Yes, sir.

ALGERNON. I shall probably not be back till Monday. You can put up my dress clothes, my smoking jacket, and all the Bunbury suits. . . .

LANE. Yes, sir. (*Handing sherry.*)

ALGERNON. I hope to-morrow will be a fine day, Lane.

LANE. It never is, sir.

ALGERNON. Lane, you're a perfect pessimist.

LANE. I do my best to give satisfaction, sir.

(*Enter* JACK. LANE *goes off.*)

JACK. There's a sensible, intellectual girl! the only girl I ever cared for in my life. (ALGERNON *is laughing immoderately.*) What on earth are you so amused at?

ALGERNON. Oh, I'm a little anxious about poor Bunbury, that's all.

JACK. If you don't take care, your friend Bunbury will get you into a serious scrape some day.

ALGERNON. I love scrapes. They are the only things that are never serious.

JACK. Oh, that's nonsense, Algy. You never talk anything but nonsense.

ALGERNON. Nobody ever does. (JACK *looks indignantly at him, and leaves the room.* ALGERNON *lights a cigarette, reads his shirt-cuff, and smiles.*)

CURTAIN

ACT II

SCENE.—*Garden at the Manor House. A flight of gray stone steps leads up to the house. The garden, an old-fashioned one, is full of roses. Time of year, July. Basket chairs, and a table covered with books, are set under a large yew tree.*

(MISS PRISM *discovered seated at the table.* CECILY *is at the back watering flowers.*)

MISS PRISM (*calling*). Cecily, Cecily! Surely such a utilitarian occupation as the watering of flowers is rather Moulton's duty than yours? Especially at a moment when intellectual pleasures await you. Your German grammar is on the table. Pray open it at page fifteen. We will repeat yesterday's lesson.

CECILY (*coming over very slowly*). But I don't like German. It isn't at all a becoming language. I know perfectly well that I look quite plain after my German lesson.

MISS PRISM. Child, you know how anxious your guardian is that you should improve yourself in every way. He laid particular stress on your German, as he was leaving for town yesterday. Indeed, he always lays stress on your German when he is leaving for town.

CECILY. Dear Uncle Jack is so very serious! Sometimes he is so serious that I think he cannot be quite well.

MISS PRISM (*drawing herself up*). Your guardian enjoys the best of health, and his gravity of demeanour is especially to be commended in one so comparatively young as he is. I know no one who has a higher sense of duty and responsibility.

CECILY. I suppose that is why he often looks a little bored when we three are together.

MISS PRISM. Cecily! I am surprised at you. Mr. Worthing has many troubles in his life. Idle merriment and triviality would be out of place in his conversation. You must remember his constant anxiety about that unfortunate young man, his brother.

CECILY. I wish Uncle Jack would allow that unfortunate young man, his brother, to come down here sometimes. We might have a good influence over him, Miss Prism. I am sure you certainly would. You know German, and geology, and things of that kind influence a man very much. (CECILY *begins to write in her diary.*)

MISS PRISM (*shaking her head*). I do not think that even I could produce any effect on a character that, according to his own brother's admission, is irretrievably weak and vacillating. Indeed, I am not sure that I would desire to reclaim him. I am not in favour of this modern mania for turning bad people into good people at a moment's notice. As a man sows so let him reap. You must put away your diary, Cecily. I really don't see why you should keep a diary at all.

CECILY. I keep a diary in order to enter the wonderful secrets of my life. If I didn't write them down I should probably forget all about them.

MISS PRISM. Memory, my dear Cecily, is the diary that we all carry about with us.

CECILY. Yes, but it usually chronicles the things that have never happened, and couldn't possibly have happened. I believe that Memory is responsible for nearly all the three-volume novels that Mudie sends us.

MISS PRISM. Do not speak slightingly of the three-volume novel, Cecily. I wrote one myself in earlier days.

CECILY. Did you really, Miss Prism? How wonderfully clever you are! I hope it did not end happily? I don't like novels that end happily. They depress me so much.

MISS PRISM. The good ended happily, and the bad unhappily. That is what Fiction means.

CECILY. I suppose so. But it seems very unfair. And was your novel ever published?

MISS PRISM. Alas! no. The manuscript unfortunately was abandoned. I use the word in the sense of lost or mislaid. To your work, child, these speculations are profitless.

CECILY (*smiling*). But I see dear Dr. Chasuble coming up through the garden.

MISS PRISM (*rising and advancing*). Dr. Chasuble! This is indeed a pleasure.

(*Enter* CANON CHASUBLE.)

CHASUBLE. And how are we this morning? Miss Prism, you are, I trust, well?

CECILY. Miss Prism has just been complaining of a slight headache. I think it would do her so much good to have a short stroll with you in the park, Dr. Chasuble.

MISS PRISM. Cecily, I have not mentioned anything about a headache.

CECILY. No, dear Miss Prism, I know that, but I felt instinctively that you had a headache. Indeed I was thinking about that, and not about my German lesson, when the Rector came in.

CHASUBLE. I hope, Cecily, you are not inattentive.

CECILY. Oh, I am afraid I am.

CHASUBLE. That is strange. Were I fortunate enough to be Miss Prism's pupil, I would hang upon her lips. (MISS PRISM *glares.*) I spoke metaphorically.—My metaphor was drawn from bees. Ahem! Mr. Worthing, I suppose, has not returned from town yet?

MISS PRISM. We do not expect him till Monday afternoon.

CHASUBLE. Ah, yes, he usually likes to spend his Sunday in London. He is not one of those whose sole aim is enjoyment, as by all accounts that unfortunate young man, his brother, seems to be. But I must not disturb Egeria and her pupil any longer.

MISS PRISM. Egeria? My name is Lætitia, Doctor.

CHASUBLE (*bowing*). A classical allusion merely, drawn from the Pagan authors. I shall see you both, no doubt, at Evensong.

MISS PRISM. I think, dear Doctor, I will have a stroll

with you. I find I have a headache after all, and a walk
might do it good.

CHASUBLE. With pleasure, Miss Prism, with pleasure.
We might go as far as the schools and back.

MISS PRISM. That would be delightful. Cecily, you will
read your Political Economy in my absence. The chapter
on the Fall of the Rupee you may omit. It is somewhat
too sensational. Even these metallic problems have
their melodramatic side.

(*Goes down the garden with* DR. CHASUBLE.)

CECILY (*picks up books and throws them back on
table*). Horrid Political Economy! Horrid Geography!
Horrid, horrid German!

(*Enter* MERRIMAN *with a card on a salver.*)

MERRIMAN. Mr. Ernest Worthing has just driven over
from the station. He has brought his luggage with him.

CECILY (*takes the card and reads it*). "Mr. Ernest
Worthing, B 4, The Albany, W." Uncle Jack's brother!
Did you tell him Mr. Worthing was in town?

MERRIMAN. Yes, miss. He seemed very much disappointed. I mentioned that you and Miss Prism were in
the garden. He said he was anxious to speak to you pri-
vately for a moment.

CECILY. Ask Mr. Ernest Worthing to come here. I suppose you had better talk to the housekeeper about a
room for him.

MERRIMAN. Yes, miss. (MERRIMAN *goes off.*)

CECILY. I have never met any really wicked person before. I feel rather frightened. I am so afraid he will look
just like everyone else.

(*Enter* ALGERNON, *very gay and debonair.*)

He does!

ALGERNON (*raising his hat*). You are my little cousin Cecily, I'm sure.

CECILY. You are under some strange mistake. I am not little. In fact, I am more than usually tall for my age. (AL-GERNON *is rather taken aback.*) But I am your cousin Cecily. You, I see from your card, are Uncle Jack's brother, my cousin Ernest, my wicked cousin Ernest.

ALGERNON. Oh! I am not really wicked at all, cousin Cecily. You mustn't think that I am wicked.

CECILY. If you are not, then you have certainly been deceiving us all in a very inexcusable manner. I hope you have not been leading a double life, pretending to be wicked and being really good all the time. That would be hypocrisy.

ALGERNON (*looks at her in amazement*). Oh! of course I have been rather reckless.

CECILY. I am glad to hear it.

ALGERNON. In fact, now you mention the subject, I have been very bad in my own small way.

CECILY. I don't think you should be so proud of that, though I am sure it must have been very pleasant.

ALGERNON. It is much pleasanter being here with you.

CECILY. I can't understand how you are here at all. Uncle Jack won't be back till Monday afternoon.

ALGERNON. That is a great disappointment. I am obliged to go up by the first train on Monday morning. I have a business appointment that I am anxious ... to miss.

CECILY. Couldn't you miss it anywhere but in London?

ALGERNON. No; the appointment is in London.

CECILY. Well, I know, of course, how important it is not to keep a business engagement, if one wants to retain any sense of the beauty of life, but still I think you had better wait till Uncle Jack arrives. I know he wants to speak to you about your emigrating.

ALGERNON. About my what?

CECILY. Your emigrating. He has gone up to buy your outfit.

ALGERNON. I certainly wouldn't let Jack buy my outfit. He has no taste in neckties at all.

CECILY. I don't think you will require neckties. Uncle Jack is sending you to Australia.

ALGERNON. Australia! I'd sooner die.

CECILY. Well, he said at dinner on Wednesday night that you would have to choose between this world, the next world, and Australia.

ALGERNON. Oh, well! The accounts I have received of Australia and the next world are not particularly encouraging. This world is good enough for me, cousin Cecily.

CECILY. Yes, but are you good enough for it?

ALGERNON. I'm afraid I'm not that. That is why I want you to reform me. You might make that your mission, if you don't mind, cousin Cecily.

CECILY. I'm afraid I've not time, this afternoon.

ALGERNON. Well, would you mind my reforming myself this afternoon?

CECILY. That is rather Quixotic of you. But I think you should try.

ALGERNON. I will. I feel better already.

CECILY. You are looking a little worse.

ALGERNON. That is because I am hungry.

CECILY. How thoughtless of me. I should have remembered that when one is going to lead an entirely new life, one requires regular and wholesome meals. Won't you come in?

ALGERNON. Thank you. Might I have a button-hole first? I never have any appetite unless I have a button-hole first.

CECILY. A Maréchal Niel? (*Picks up scissors.*)

ALGERNON. No, I'd sooner have a pink rose.

CECILY. Why? (*Cuts a flower.*)

ALGERNON. Because you are like a pink rose, cousin Cecily.

CECILY. I don't think it can be right for you to talk to me like that. Miss Prism never says such things to me.

ALGERNON. Then Miss Prism is a short-sighted old lady. (CECILY *puts the rose in his button-hole.*) You are the prettiest girl I ever saw.

CECILY. Miss Prism says that all good looks are a snare.

ALGERNON. They are a snare that every sensible man would like to be caught in.

CECILY. Oh! I don't think I would care to catch a sensible man. I shouldn't know what to talk to him about.

(*They pass into the house.* MISS PRISM *and* DR. CHA-
SUBLE *return.*)

MISS PRISM. You are too much alone, dear Dr. Chasuble. You should get married. A misanthrope I can understand—a womanthrope, never!

CHASUBLE (*with a scholar's shudder*). Believe me, I do not deserve so neologistic a phrase. The precept as well as the practice of the Primitive Church was distinctly against matrimony.

MISS PRISM (*sententiously*). That is obviously the reason why the Primitive Church has not lasted up to the present day. And you do not seem to realize, dear Doctor, that by persistently remaining single, a man converts himself into a permanent public temptation. Men should be careful; this very celibacy leads weaker vessels astray.

CHASUBLE. But is a man not equally attractive when married?

MISS PRISM. No married man is ever attractive except to his wife.

CHASUBLE. And often, I've been told, not even to her.

MISS PRISM. That depends on the intellectual sympathies of the woman. Maturity can always be depended on. Ripeness can be trusted. Young women are green.

(DR. CHASUBLE *starts.*) I spoke horticulturally. My metaphor was drawn from fruits. But where is Cecily?

CHASUBLE. Perhaps she followed us to the schools.

(Enter JACK slowly from the back of the garden. He is dressed in the deepest mourning, with crepe hatband and black gloves.)

MISS PRISM. Mr. Worthing!

CHASUBLE. Mr. Worthing?

MISS PRISM. This is indeed a surprise. We did not look for you till Monday afternoon.

JACK (*shakes MISS PRISM's hand in a tragic manner*). I have returned sooner than I expected. Dr. Chasuble, I hope you are well?

CHASUBLE. Dear Mr. Worthing, I trust this garb of woe does not betoken some terrible calamity?

JACK. My brother.

MISS PRISM. More shameful debts and extravagance?

CHASUBLE. Still leading his life of pleasure?

JACK (*shaking his head*). Dead!

CHASUBLE. Your brother Ernest dead?

JACK. Quite dead.

MISS PRISM. What a lesson for him! I trust he will profit by it.

CHASUBLE. Mr. Worthing, I offer you my sincere condolence. You have at least the consolation of knowing that you were always the most generous and forgiving of brothers.

JACK. Poor Ernest! He had many faults, but it is a sad, sad blow.

CHASUBLE. Very sad indeed. Were you with him at the end?

JACK. No. He died abroad; in Paris, in fact. I had a telegram last night from the manager of the Grand Hotel.

CHASUBLE. Was the cause of death mentioned?

JACK. A severe chill, it seems.

MISS PRISM. As a man sows, so shall he reap.

CHASUBLE (*raising his hand*). Charity, dear Miss Prism, charity! None of us are perfect. I myself am peculiarly susceptible to draughts. Will the interment take place here?

JACK. No. He seems to have expressed a desire to be buried in Paris.

CHASUBLE. In Paris! (*Shakes his head.*) I fear that hardly points to any very serious state of mind at the last. You would no doubt wish me to make some slight allusion to this tragic domestic affliction next Sunday. (JACK *presses his hand convulsively.*) My sermon on the meaning of the manna in the wilderness can be adapted to almost any occasion, joyful, or, as in the present case, distressing. (*All sigh.*) I have preached it at harvest celebrations, christenings, confirmations, on days of humiliation and festal days. The last time I delivered it was in the Cathedral, as a charity sermon on behalf of the Society for the Prevention of Discontentment Among the Upper Orders. The Bishop, who was present, was much struck by some of the analogies I drew.

JACK. Ah, that reminds me, you mentioned christenings I think, Dr. Chasuble? I suppose you know how to christen all right? (DR. CHASUBLE *looks astounded.*) I mean, of course, you are continually christening, aren't you?

MISS PRISM. It is, I regret to say, one of the Rector's most constant duties in this parish. I have often spoken to the poorer classes on the subject. But they don't seem to know what thrift is.

CHASUBLE. But is there any particular infant in whom you are interested, Mr. Worthing? Your brother was, I believe, unmarried, was he not?

JACK. Oh, yes.

MISS PRISM (*bitterly*). People who live entirely for pleasure usually are.

JACK. But it is not for any child, dear Doctor. I am very fond of children. No! the fact is, I would like to be christened myself, this afternoon, if you have nothing better to do.

CHASUBLE. But surely, Mr. Worthing, you have been christened already?

JACK. I don't remember anything about it.

CHASUBLE. But have you any grave doubts on the subject?

JACK. I certainly intend to have. Of course, I don't know if the thing would bother you in any way, or if you think I am a little too old now.

CHASUBLE. Not at all. The sprinkling, and, indeed, the immersion of adults is a perfectly canonical practice.

JACK. Immersion!

CHASUBLE. You need have no apprehensions. Sprinkling is all that is necessary, or indeed I think advisable. Our weather is so changeable. At what hour would you wish the ceremony performed?

JACK. Oh, I might trot around about five if that would suit you.

CHASUBLE. Perfectly, perfectly! In fact I have two similar ceremonies to perform at that time. A case of twins that occurred recently in one of the outlying cottages on your own estate. Poor Jenkins the carter, a most hard-working man.

JACK. Oh! I don't see much fun in being christened along with other babies. It would be childish. Would half-past five do?

CHASUBLE. Admirably! Admirably! (*Takes out watch.*) And now, dear Mr. Worthing, I will not intrude any longer into a house of sorrow. I would merely beg you not to be too much bowed down by grief. What seem to us bitter trials at the moment are often blessings in disguise.

MISS PRISM. This seems to me a blessing of an extremely obvious kind.

(*Enter* CECILY *from the house.*)

CECILY. Uncle Jack! Oh, I am pleased to see you back. But what horrid clothes you have on! Do go and change them.

MISS PRISM. Cecily!

CHASUBLE. My child! my child! (CECILY *goes towards* JACK; *he kisses her brow in a melancholy manner.*)

CECILY. What is the matter, Uncle Jack? Do look happy! You look as if you had a toothache and I have such a surprise for you. Who do you think is in the dining-room? Your brother!

JACK. Who?

CECILY. Your brother, Ernest. He arrived about half an hour ago.

JACK. What nonsense! I haven't got a brother.

CECILY. Oh, don't say that. However badly he may have behaved to you in the past he is still your brother. You couldn't be so heartless as to disown him. I'll tell him to come out. And you will shake hands with him, won't you, Uncle Jack? (*Runs back into the house.*)

CHASUBLE. These are very joyful tidings.

MISS PRISM. After we had all been resigned to his loss, his sudden return seems to me peculiarly distressing.

JACK. My brother is in the dining-room? I don't know what it all means. I think it is perfectly absurd.

(*Enter* ALGERNON *and* CECILY *hand in hand. They come slowly up to* JACK.)

JACK. Good heavens! (*Motions* ALGERNON *away.*)

ALGERNON. Brother John, I have come down from town to tell you that I am very sorry for all the trouble I have given you, and that I intend to lead a better life in the future. (JACK *glares at him and does not take his hand.*)

CECILY. Uncle Jack, you are not going to refuse your own brother's hand.

JACK. Nothing will induce me to take his hand. I think his coming down here disgraceful. He knows perfectly well why.

CECILY. Uncle Jack, do be nice. There is good in every-one. Ernest has just been telling me about his poor invalid friend, Mr. Bunbury, whom he goes to visit so often. And surely there must be much good in one who is kind to an invalid, and leaves the pleasures of London to sit by a bed of pain.

JACK. Oh, he has been talking about Bunbury, has he?

CECILY. Yes, he has told me all about poor Mr. Bunbury, and his terrible state of health.

JACK. Bunbury! Well, I won't have him talk to you about Bunbury or about anything else. It is enough to drive one perfectly frantic.

ALGERNON. Of course I admit that the faults were all on my side. But I must say that I think that Brother John's coldness to me is peculiarly painful. I expected a more enthusiastic welcome, especially considering it is the first time I have come here.

CECILY. Uncle Jack, if you don't shake hands with Er-nest I will never forgive you.

JACK. Never forgive me?

CECILY. Never, never, never!

JACK. Well, this is the last time I shall ever do it. (*Shakes hands with* ALGERNON *and glares.*)

CHASUBLE. It's pleasant, is it not, to see so perfect a reconciliation? I think we might leave the two brothers together.

MISS PRISM. Cecily, you will come with us.

CECILY. Certainly, Miss Prism. My little task of recon-ciliation is over.

CHASUBLE. You have done a beautiful action to-day, dear child.

MISS PRISM. We must not be premature in our judgments.

CECILY. I feel very happy. (*They all go off.*)

JACK. You young scoundrel, Algy, you must get out of this place as soon as possible. I don't allow any Bunburying here.

(*Enter* MERRIMAN.)

MERRIMAN. I have put Mr. Ernest's things in the room next to yours, sir. I suppose that is all right?

JACK. What?

MERRIMAN. Mr. Ernest's luggage, sir. I have unpacked it and put it in the room next to your own.

JACK. His luggage?

MERRIMAN. Yes, sir. Three portmanteaus, a dressing-case, two hat-boxes, and a large luncheon-basket.

ALGERNON. I am afraid I can't stay more than a week this time.

JACK. Merriman, order the dog-cart at once. Mr. Ernest has been suddenly called back to town.

MERRIMAN. Yes, sir. (*Goes back into the house.*)

ALGERNON. What a fearful liar you are, Jack. I have not been called back to town at all.

JACK. Yes, you have.

ALGERNON. I haven't heard anyone call me.

JACK. Your duty as a gentleman calls you back.

ALGERNON. My duty as a gentleman has never interfered with my pleasures in the smallest degree.

JACK. I can quite understand that.

ALGERNON. Well, Cecily is a darling.

JACK. You are not to talk of Miss Cardew like that. I don't like it.

ALGERNON. Well, I don't like your clothes. You look perfectly ridiculous in them. Why on earth don't you go up and change? It is perfectly childish to be in deep mourning for a man who is actually staying for a whole week with you in your house as a guest. I call it grotesque.

JACK. You are certainly not staying with me for a

whole week as a guest or anything else. You have got to leave ... by the four-five train.

ALGERNON. I certainly won't leave you so long as you are in mourning. It would be most unfriendly. If I were in mourning you would stay with me, I suppose. I should think it very unkind if you didn't.

JACK. Well, will you go if I change my clothes?

ALGERNON. Yes, if you are not too long. I never saw anybody take so long to dress, and with such little result.

JACK. Well, at any rate, that is better than being always over-dressed as you are.

ALGERNON. If I am occasionally a little over-dressed, I make up for it by being always immensely over-educated.

JACK. Your vanity is ridiculous, your conduct an outrage, and your presence in my garden utterly absurd. However, you have got to catch the four-five, and I hope you will have a pleasant journey back to town. This Bunburying, as you call it, has not been a great success for you. (*Goes into the house.*)

ALGERNON. I think it has been a great success. I'm in love with Cecily, and that is everything. (*Enter CECILY at the back of the garden. She picks up the can and begins to water the flowers.*) But I must see her before I go, and make arrangements for another Bunbury. Ah, there she is.

CECILY. Oh, I merely came back to water the roses. I thought you were with Uncle Jack.

ALGERNON. He's gone to order the dog-cart for me.

CECILY. Oh, is he going to take you for a nice drive?

ALGERNON. He's going to send me away.

CECILY. Then have we got to part?

ALGERNON. I am afraid so. It's a very painful parting.

CECILY. It is always painful to part from people whom one has known for a very brief space of time. The absence of old friends one can endure with equanimity. But even a momentary separation from anyone to whom one has just been introduced is almost unbearable.

ALGERNON. Thank you.

(*Enter* MERRIMAN.)

MERRIMAN. The dog-cart is at the door, sir. (ALGERNON *looks appealingly at* CECILY.)

CECILY. It can wait, Merriman . . . for . . . five minutes.

MERRIMAN. Yes, miss. (*Exit* MERRIMAN.)

ALGERNON. I hope, Cecily, I shall not offend you if I state quite frankly and openly that you seem to me to be in every way the visible personification of absolute perfection.

CECILY. I think your frankness does you great credit, Ernest. If you will allow me I will copy your remarks into my diary. (*Goes over to table and begins writing in diary.*)

ALGERNON. Do you really keep a diary? I'd give anything to look at it. May I?

CECILY. Oh, no. (*Puts her hand over it.*) You see, it is simply a very young girl's record of her own thoughts and impressions, and consequently meant for publication. When it appears in volume form I hope you will order a copy. But pray, Ernest, don't stop. I delight in taking down from dictation. I have reached "absolute perfection." You can go on. I am quite ready for more.

ALGERNON (*somewhat taken aback*). Ahem! Ahem!

CECILY. Oh, don't cough, Ernest. When one is dictating one should speak fluently and not cough. Besides, I don't know how to spell a cough. (*Writes as* ALGERNON *speaks.*)

ALGERNON (*speaking very rapidly*). Cecily, ever since I first looked upon your wonderful and incomparable beauty, I have dared to love you wildly, passionately, devotedly, hopelessly.

CECILY. I don't think that you should tell me that you love me wildly, passionately, devotedly, hopelessly. Hopelessly doesn't seem to make much sense, does it?

ALGERNON. Cecily!

(*Enter* MERRIMAN.)

MERRIMAN. The dog-cart is waiting, sir.

ALGERNON. Tell it to come round next week, at the same hour.

MERRIMAN (*looks at* CECILY, *who makes no sign*). Yes, sir.

(MERRIMAN *retires.*)

CECILY. Uncle Jack would be very much annoyed if he knew you were staying on till next week, at the same hour.

ALGERNON. Oh, I don't care about Jack. I don't care for anybody in the whole world but you. I love you, Cecily. You will marry me, won't you?

CECILY. You silly you! Of course. Why, we have been engaged for the last three months.

ALGERNON. For the last three months?

CECILY. Yes, it will be exactly three months on Thursday.

ALGERNON. But how did we become engaged?

CECILY. Well, ever since dear Uncle Jack first confessed to us that he had a younger brother who was very wicked and bad, you of course have formed the chief topic of conversation between myself and Miss Prism. And of course a man who is much talked about is always very attractive. One feels there must be something in him after all. I daresay it was foolish of me, but I fell in love with you, Ernest.

ALGERNON. Darling! And when was the engagement actually settled?

CECILY. On the 14th of February last. Worn out by your entire ignorance of my existence, I determined to end the matter one way or the other, and after a long struggle with myself I accepted you under this dear old tree here. The next day I bought this little ring in your name, and this is the little bangle with the true lovers' knot I promised you always to wear.

ALGERNON. Did I give you this? It's very pretty, isn't it?

CECILY. Yes, you've wonderfully good taste, Ernest. It's the excuse I've always given for your leading such a bad life. And this is the box in which I keep all your dear letters. (*Kneels at table, opens box, and produces letters tied up with blue ribbon.*)

ALGERNON. My letters! But my own sweet Cecily, I have never written you any letters.

CECILY. You need hardly remind me of that, Ernest. I remember only too well that I was forced to write your letters for you. I wrote always three times a week, and sometimes oftener.

ALGERNON. Oh, do let me read them, Cecily?

CECILY. Oh, I couldn't possibly. They would make you far too conceited. (*Replaces box.*) The three you wrote me after I had broken off the engagement are so beautiful, and so badly spelled, that even now I can hardly read them without crying a little.

ALGERNON. But was our engagement ever broken off?

CECILY. Of course it was. On the 22nd of last March. You can see the entry if you like. (*Shows diary.*) "Today I broke off my engagement with Ernest. I feel it is better to do so. The weather still continues charming."

ALGERNON. But why on earth did you break it off? What had I done? I had done nothing at all, Cecily. I am very much hurt indeed to hear you broke it off. Particularly when the weather was so charming.

CECILY. It would hardly have been a really serious engagement if it hadn't been broken off at least once. But I forgave you before the week was out.

ALGERNON (*crossing to her, and kneeling*). What a perfect angel you are, Cecily.

CECILY. You dear romantic boy. (*He kisses her; she puts her fingers through his hair.*) I hope your hair curls naturally, does it?

ALGERNON. Yes, darling, with a little help from others.

CECILY. I am so glad.

ALGERNON. You'll never break off our engagement again, Cecily?

CECILY. I don't think I could break it off now that I have actually met you. Besides, of course, there is the question of your name.

ALGERNON. Yes, of course. (*Nervously.*)

CECILY. You must not laugh at me, darling, but it has always been a girlish dream of mine to love some one whose name was Ernest. (ALGERNON *rises,* CECILY *also.*) There is something in that name that seems to inspire absolute confidence. I pity any poor married woman whose husband is not called Ernest.

ALGERNON. But, my dear child, do you mean to say you could not love me if I had some other name?

CECILY. But what name?

ALGERNON. Oh, any name you like—Algernon, for instance. . . .

CECILY. But I don't like the name of Algernon.

ALGERNON. Well, my own dear, sweet, loving little darling, I really can't see why you should object to the name of Algernon. It is not at all a bad name. In fact, it is rather an aristocratic name. Half of the chaps who get into the Bankruptcy Court are called Algernon. But seriously, Cecily . . . (*moving to her*) . . . if my name was Algy, couldn't you love me?

CECILY. I might respect you, Ernest, I might admire your character, but I fear that I should not be able to give you my undivided attention.

ALGERNON. Ahem! Cecily! (*Picking up hat.*) Your Rector here is, I suppose, thoroughly experienced in the practice of all the rites and ceremonials of the church?

CECILY. Oh, yes. Dr. Chasuble is a most learned man. He has never written a single book, so you can imagine how much he knows.

ALGERNON. I must see him at once on a most important christening—I mean on most important business.

CECILY. Oh!

ALGERNON. I sha'n't be away more than half an hour.

CECILY. Considering that we have been engaged since February the 14th, and that I only met you to-day for the first time, I think it is rather hard that you should leave me for so long a period as half an hour. Couldn't you make it twenty minutes?

ALGERNON. I'll be back in no time. (*Kisses her and rushes down the garden.*)

CECILY. What an impetuous boy he is. I like his hair so much. I must enter his proposal in my diary.

(*Enter* MERRIMAN.)

MERRIMAN. A Miss Fairfax has just called to see Mr. Worthing. On very important business, Miss Fairfax states.

CECILY. Isn't Mr. Worthing in his library?

MERRIMAN. Mr. Worthing went over in the direction of the Rectory some time ago.

CECILY. Pray ask the lady to come out here; Mr. Worthing is sure to be back soon. And you can bring tea.

MERRIMAN. Yes, miss. (*Goes out.*)

CECILY. Miss Fairfax! I suppose one of the many good elderly women who are associated with Uncle Jack in some of his philanthropic work in London. I don't quite like women who are interested in philanthropic work. I think it is so forward of them.

(*Enter* MERRIMAN.)

MERRIMAN. Miss Fairfax.

(*Enter* GWENDOLEN. *Exit* MERRIMAN.)

CECILY (*advancing to meet her*). Pray let me introduce myself to you. My name is Cecily Cardew.

GWENDOLEN. Cecily Cardew? (*Moving to her and*

shaking hands.) What a very sweet name! Something tells me that we are going to be great friends. I like you already more than I can say. My first impressions of people are never wrong.

CECILY. How nice of you to like me so much after we have known each other such a comparatively short time. Pray sit down.

GWENDOLEN (*still standing up*). I may call you Cecily, may I not?

CECILY. With pleasure!

GWENDOLEN. And you will always call me Gwendolen, won't you?

CECILY. If you wish.

GWENDOLEN. Then that is all quite settled, is it not?

CECILY. I hope so. (*A pause. They both sit down together.*)

GWENDOLEN. Perhaps this might be a favourable opportunity for my mentioning who I am. My father is Lord Bracknell. You have never heard of Papa, I suppose?

CECILY. I don't think so.

GWENDOLEN. Outside the family circle, Papa, I am glad to say, is entirely unknown. I think that is quite as it should be. The home seems to me to be the proper sphere for the man. And certainly once a man begins to neglect his domestic duties he becomes painfully effeminate, does he not? And I don't like that. It makes men so very attractive. Cecily, Mamma, whose views on education are remarkably strict, has brought me up to be extremely short-sighted; it is part of her system; so do you mind my looking at you through my glasses?

CECILY. Oh, not at all, Gwendolen. I am very fond of being looked at.

GWENDOLEN (*after examining* CECILY *carefully through a lorgnette*). You are here on a short visit, I suppose.

CECILY. Oh, no, I live here.

GWENDOLEN (*severely*). Really? Your mother, no doubt, or some female relative of advanced years, resides here also?

CECILY. Oh, no. I have no mother, nor, in fact, any relations.

GWENDOLEN. Indeed?

CECILY. My dear guardian, with the assistance of Miss Prism, has the arduous task of looking after me.

GWENDOLEN. Your guardian?

CECILY. Yes, I am Mr. Worthing's ward.

GWENDOLEN. Oh! It is strange he never mentioned to me that he had a ward. How secretive of him! He grows more interesting hourly. I am not sure, however, that the news inspires me with feelings of unmixed delight. (*Rising and going to her.*) I am very fond of you, Cecily; I have liked you ever since I met you. But I am bound to state that now that I know that you are Mr. Worthing's ward, I cannot help expressing a wish you were—well, just a little older than you seem to be—and not quite so very alluring in appearance. In fact, if I may speak candidly—

CECILY. Pray do! I think that whenever one has anything unpleasant to say, one should always be quite candid.

GWENDOLEN. Well, to speak with perfect candour, Cecily, I wish that you were fully forty-two, and more than usually plain for your age. Ernest has a strong upright nature. He is the very soul of truth and honour. Disloyalty would be as impossible to him as deception. But even men of the noblest possible moral character are extremely susceptible to the influence of the physical charms of others. Modern, no less than Ancient, History supplies us with many most painful examples of what I refer to. If it were not so, indeed, History would be quite unreadable.

CECILY. I beg your pardon, Gwendolen, did you say Ernest?

GWENDOLEN. Yes.

CECILY. Oh, but it is not Mr. Ernest Worthing who is my guardian. It is his brother—his elder brother.

GWENDOLEN (*sitting down again*). Ernest never mentioned to me that he had a brother.

CECILY. I am sorry to say they have not been on good terms for a long time.

GWENDOLEN. Ah! that accounts for it. And now that I think of it I have never heard any man mention his brother. The subject seems distasteful to most men. Cecily, you have lifted a load from my mind. I was growing almost anxious. It would have been terrible if any cloud had come across a friendship like ours, would it not? Of course you are quite, quite sure that it is not Mr. Ernest Worthing who is your guardian?

CECILY. Quite sure. (*A pause.*) In fact, I am going to be his.

GWENDOLEN (*enquiringly*). I beg your pardon?

CECILY (*rather shy and confidingly*). Dearest Gwendolen, there is no reason why I should make a secret of it to you. Our little county newspaper is sure to chronicle the fact next week. Mr. Ernest Worthing and I are engaged to be married.

GWENDOLEN (*quite politely, rising*). My darling Cecily, I think there must be some slight error. Mr. Ernest Worthing is engaged to me. The announcement will appear in the *Morning Post* on Saturday at the latest.

CECILY (*very politely, rising*). I am afraid you must be under some misconception. Ernest proposed to me exactly ten minutes ago. (*Shows diary.*)

GWENDOLEN (*examines diary through her lorgnette carefully*). It is certainly very curious, for he asked me to be his wife yesterday afternoon at 5:30. If you would care to verify the incident, pray do so. (*Produces diary of her own.*) I never travel without my diary. One should always have something sensational to read in the train. I am so sorry, dear Cecily, if it is any disappointment to you, but I am afraid *I* have the prior claim.

CECILY. It would distress me more than I can tell you, dear Gwendolen, if it caused you any mental or physical anguish, but I feel bound to point out that since Ernest proposed to you he clearly has changed his mind.

GWENDOLEN (*meditatively*). If the poor fellow has been entrapped into any foolish promise I shall consider it my duty to rescue him at once, and with a firm hand.

CECILY (*thoughtfully and sadly*). Whatever unfortunate entanglement my dear boy may have got into, I will never reproach him with it after we are married.

GWENDOLEN. Do you allude to me, Miss Cardew, as an entanglement? You are presumptuous. On an occasion of this kind it becomes more than a moral duty to speak one's mind. It becomes a pleasure.

CECILY. Do you suggest, Miss Fairfax, that I entrapped Ernest into an engagement? How dare you? This is no time for wearing the shallow mask of manners. When I see a spade I call it a spade.

GWENDOLEN (*satirically*). I am glad to say that I have never seen a spade. It is obvious that our social spheres have been widely different.

(*Enter* MERRIMAN, *followed by the footman. He carries a salver, tablecloth, and plate-stand.* CECILY *is about to retort. The presence of the servants exercises a restraining influence, under which both girls chafe.*)

MERRIMAN. Shall I lay tea here as usual, miss?

CECILY (*sternly, in a calm voice*). Yes, as usual. (MERRIMAN *begins to clear and lay cloth. A long pause.* CECILY *and* GWENDOLEN *glare at each other.*)

GWENDOLEN. Are there many interesting walks in the vicinity, Miss Cardew?

CECILY. Oh, yes, a great many. From the top of one of the hills quite close one can see five counties.

GWENDOLEN. Five counties! I don't think I should like that. I hate crowds.

CECILY (*sweetly*). I suppose that is why you live in town? (GWENDOLEN *bites her lip, and beats her foot nervously with her parasol.*)

GWENDOLEN (*looking round*). Quite a well-kept garden this is, Miss Cardew.

CECILY. So glad you like it, Miss Fairfax.

GWENDOLEN. I had no idea there were any flowers in the country.

CECILY. Oh, flowers are as common here, Miss Fairfax, as people are in London.

GWENDOLEN. Personally I cannot understand how anybody manages to exist in the country, if anybody who is anybody does. The country always bores me to death.

CECILY. Ah! This is what the newspapers call agricultural depression, is it not? I believe the aristocracy are suffering very much from it just at present. It is almost an epidemic amongst them, I have been told. May I offer you some tea, Miss Fairfax?

GWENDOLEN (*with elaborate politeness*). Thank you. (*Aside.*) Detestable girl! But I require tea!

CECILY (*sweetly*). Sugar?

GWENDOLEN (*superciliously*). No, thank you. Sugar is not fashionable any more. (CECILY *looks angrily at her, takes up the tongs, and puts four lumps of sugar into the cup.*)

CECILY (*severely*). Cake or bread and butter?

GWENDOLEN (*in a bored manner*). Bread and butter, please. Cake is rarely seen at the best houses now-a-days.

CECILY (*cuts a very large slice of cake, and puts it on the tray*). Hand that to Miss Fairfax. (MERRIMAN *does so, and goes out with footman.* GWENDOLEN *drinks the tea and makes a grimace. Puts down cup at once, reaches out her hand to the bread and butter, looks at it, and finds it is cake. Rises in indignation.*)

GWENDOLEN. You have filled my tea with lumps of sugar, and though I asked most distinctly for bread and butter, you have given me cake. I am known for the gentleness of my disposition, and the extraordinary sweetness of my nature, but I warn you, Miss Cardew, you may go too far.

CECILY (*rising*). To save my poor, innocent, trusting boy from the machinations of any other girl there are no lengths to which I would not go.

GWENDOLEN. From the moment I saw you I distrusted you. I felt that you were false and deceitful. I am never deceived in such matters. My first impressions of people are invariably right.

CECILY. It seems to me, Miss Fairfax, that I am trespassing on your valuable time. No doubt you have many other calls of a similar character to make in the neighbourhood.

(*Enter* JACK.)

GWENDOLEN (*catching sight of him*). Ernest! My own Ernest!

JACK. Gwendolen! Darling! (*Offers to kiss her.*)

GWENDOLEN (*drawing back*). A moment! May I ask if you are engaged to be married to this young lady? (*Points to* CECILY.)

JACK (*laughing*). To dear little Cecily! Of course not! What could have put such an idea into your pretty little head?

GWENDOLEN. Thank you. You may. (*Offers her cheek.*)

CECILY (*very sweetly*). I knew there must be some misunderstanding, Miss Fairfax. The gentleman whose arm is at present around your waist is my dear guardian, Mr. John Worthing.

GWENDOLEN. I beg your pardon?

CECILY. This is Uncle Jack.

GWENDOLEN (*receding*). Jack! Oh!

(*Enter* ALGERNON.)

CECILY. Here is Ernest.

ALGERNON (*goes straight over to* CECILY *without noticing anyone else*). My own love! (*Offers to kiss her.*)

CECILY (*drawing back*). A moment, Ernest! May I ask you—are you engaged to be married to this young lady?

ALGERNON (*looking round*). To what young lady? Good heavens! Gwendolen!

CECILY. Yes, to good heavens, Gwendolen, I mean to Gwendolen.

ALGERNON (*laughing*). Of course not! What could have put such an idea into your pretty little head?

CECILY. Thank you. (*Presenting her cheek to be kissed.*) You may. (ALGERNON *kisses her.*)

GWENDOLEN. I felt there was some slight error, Miss Cardew. The gentleman who is now embracing you is my cousin, Mr. Algernon Moncrieff.

CECILY (*breaking away from* ALGERNON). Algernon Moncrieff! Oh! (*The two girls move towards each other and put their arms round each other's waists as if for protection.*)

CECILY. Are you called Algernon?

ALGERNON. I cannot deny it.

CECILY. Oh!

GWENDOLEN. Is your name really John?

JACK (*standing rather proudly*). I could deny it if I liked. I could deny anything if I liked. But my name certainly is John. It has been John for years.

CECILY (*to* GWENDOLEN). A gross deception has been practised on both of us.

GWENDOLEN. My poor wounded Cecily!

CECILY. My sweet, wronged Gwendolen!

GWENDOLEN (*slowly and seriously*). You will call me sister, will you not? (*They embrace.* JACK *and* ALGERNON *groan and walk up and down.*)

CECILY (*rather brightly*). There is just one question I would like to be allowed to ask my guardian.

GWENDOLEN. An admirable idea! Mr. Worthing, there

is just one question I would like to be permitted to put
to you. Where is your brother Ernest? We are both engaged to be married to your brother Ernest, so it is a
matter of some importance to us to know where your
brother Ernest is at present.

JACK (*slowly and hesitatingly*). Gwendolen—Cecily—it
is very painful for me to be forced to speak the truth. It
is the first time in my life that I have ever been reduced
to such a painful position, and I am really quite inexperi-
enced in doing anything of the kind. However, I will tell
you quite frankly that I have no brother Ernest. I have
no brother at all. I never had a brother in my life, and I
certainly have not the smallest intention of ever having
one in the future.

CECILY (*surprised*). No brother at all?

JACK (*cheerily*). None!

GWENDOLEN (*severely*). Had you never a brother of
any kind?

JACK (*pleasantly*). Never. Not even of any kind.

GWENDOLEN. I am afraid it is quite clear, Cecily, that
neither of us is engaged to be married to anyone.

CECILY. It is not a very pleasant position for a young
girl suddenly to find herself in, is it?

GWENDOLEN. Let us go into the house. They will
hardly venture to come after us there.

CECILY. No, men are so cowardly, aren't they? (*They
retire into the house with scornful looks.*)

JACK. This ghastly state of things is what you call Bunburying, I suppose?

ALGERNON. Yes, and a perfectly wonderful Bunbury
it is. The most wonderful Bunbury I have ever had in
my life.

JACK. Well, you've no right whatsoever to Bunbury
here.

ALGERNON. That is absurd. One has a right to Bunbury anywhere one chooses. Every serious Bunburyist
knows that.

JACK. Serious Bunburyist! Good heavens!

ALGERNON. Well, one must be serious about something, if one wants to have any amusement in life. I happen to be serious about Bunburying. What on earth you are serious about I haven't got the remotest idea. About everything, I should fancy. You have such an absolutely trivial nature.

JACK. Well, the only small satisfaction I have in the whole of this wretched business is that your friend Bunbury is quite exploded. You won't be able to run down to the country quite so often as you used to do, dear Algy. And a very good thing, too.

ALGERNON. Your brother is a little off colour, isn't he, dear Jack? You won't be able to disappear to London quite so frequently as your wicked custom was. And not a bad thing, either.

JACK. As for your conduct towards Miss Cardew, I must say that your taking in a sweet, simple, innocent girl like that is quite inexcusable. To say nothing of the fact that she is my ward.

ALGERNON. I can see no possible defence at all for your deceiving a brilliant, clever, thoroughly experienced young lady like Miss Fairfax. To say nothing of the fact that she is my cousin.

JACK. I wanted to be engaged to Gwendolen, that is all. I love her.

ALGERNON. Well, I simply wanted to be engaged to Cecily. I adore her.

JACK. There is certainly no chance of your marrying Miss Cardew.

ALGERNON. I don't think there is much likelihood, Jack, of you and Miss Fairfax being united.

JACK. Well, that is no business of yours.

ALGERNON. If it was my business, I wouldn't talk about it. (*Begins to eat muffins.*) It is very vulgar to talk about one's business. Only people like stock-brokers do that, and then merely at dinner parties.

JACK. How you can sit there, calmly eating muffins, when we are in this horrible trouble, I can't make out. You seem to me to be perfectly heartless.

ALGERNON. Well, I can't eat muffins in an agitated manner. The butter would probably get on my cuffs. One should always eat muffins quite calmly. It is the only way to eat them.

JACK. I say it's perfectly heartless your eating muffins at all, under the circumstances.

ALGERNON. When I am in trouble, eating is the only thing that consoles me. Indeed, when I am in really great trouble, as anyone who knows me intimately will tell you, I refuse everything except food and drink. At the present moment I am eating muffins because I am unhappy. Besides, I am particularly fond of muffins. (*Rising.*)

JACK (*rising*). Well, that is no reason why you should eat them all in that greedy way. (*Takes muffin from* ALGERNON.)

ALGERNON (*offering tea-cake*). I wish you would have tea-cake instead. I don't like tea-cake.

JACK. Good heavens! I suppose a man may eat his own muffins in his own garden.

ALGERNON. But you have just said it was perfectly heartless to eat muffins.

JACK. I said it was perfectly heartless of you, under the circumstances. That is a very different thing.

ALGERNON. That may be. But the muffins are the same. (*He seizes the muffin dish from* JACK.)

JACK. Algy, I wish to goodness you would go.

ALGERNON. You can't possibly ask me to go without having some dinner. It's absurd. I never go without my dinner. No one ever does, except vegetarians and people like that. Besides, I have just made arrangements with Dr. Chasuble to be christened at a quarter to six under the name of Ernest.

JACK. My dear fellow, the sooner you give up that nonsense the better. I made arrangements this morning with Chasuble to be christened myself at 5:30, and I naturally will take the name of Ernest. Gwendolen would wish it. We can't both be christened Ernest. It's absurd. Besides, I have a perfect right to be christened if I like. There is no evidence at all that I ever have been christened by anybody. I should think it extremely probable I never was, and so does Dr. Chasuble. It is entirely different in your case. You have been christened already.

ALGERNON. Yes, but I have not been christened for years.

JACK. Yes, but you have been christened. That is the important thing.

ALGERNON. Quite so. So I know my constitution can stand it. If you are not quite sure about your ever having been christened, I must say I think it rather dangerous your venturing on it now. It might make you very unwell. You can hardly have forgotten that someone very closely connected with you was very nearly carried off this week in Paris by a severe chill.

JACK. Yes, but you said yourself that a severe chill was not hereditary.

ALGERNON. It usedn't to be, I know—but I daresay it is now. Science is always making wonderful improvements in things.

JACK (picking up the muffin dish). Oh, that is nonsense; you are always talking nonsense.

ALGERNON. Jack, you are at the muffins again! I wish you wouldn't. There are only two left. (Takes them.) I told you I was particularly fond of muffins.

JACK. But I hate tea-cake.

ALGERNON. Why on earth then do you allow tea-cake to be served up for your guests? What ideas you have of hospitality!

JACK. Algernon! I have already told you to go. I don't want you here. Why don't you go?

ALGERNON. I haven't quite finished my tea yet, and

there is still one muffin left. (JACK *groans, and sinks into a chair.* ALGERNON *still continues eating.*)

CURTAIN

ACT III

SCENE.—*Morning-room at the Manor House.* GWENDOLEN *and* CECILY *are at the window, looking out into the garden.*

GWENDOLEN. The fact that they did not follow us at once into the house, as anyone else would have done, seems to me to show that they have some sense of shame left.

CECILY. They have been eating muffins. That looks like repentance.

GWENDOLEN (*after a pause*). They don't seem to notice us at all. Couldn't you cough?

CECILY. But I haven't got a cough.

GWENDOLEN. They're looking at us. What effrontery!

CECILY. They're approaching. That's very forward of them.

GWENDOLEN. Let us preserve a dignified silence.

CECILY. Certainly, it's the only thing to do now.

(*Enter* JACK, *followed by* ALGERNON. *They whistle some dreadful popular air from a British opera.*)

GWENDOLEN. This dignified silence seems to produce an unpleasant effect.

CECILY. A most distasteful one.

GWENDOLEN. But we will not be the first to speak.

CECILY. Certainly not.

GWENDOLEN. Mr. Worthing, I have something very particular to ask you. Much depends on your reply.

CECILY. Gwendolen, your common sense is invaluable. Mr. Moncrieff, kindly answer me the following question. Why did you pretend to be my guardian's brother?

ALGERNON. In order that I might have an opportunity of meeting you.

CECILY (*to* GWENDOLEN). That certainly seems a satisfactory explanation, does it not?

GWENDOLEN. Yes, dear, if you can believe him.

CECILY. I don't. But that does not affect the wonderful beauty of his answer.

GWENDOLEN. True. In matters of grave importance, style, not sincerity, is the vital thing. Mr. Worthing, what explanation can you offer to me for pretending to have a brother? Was it in order that you might have an opportunity of coming up to town to see me as often as possible?

JACK. Can you doubt it, Miss Fairfax?

GWENDOLEN. I have the gravest doubts upon the subject. But I intend to crush them. This is not the moment for German scepticism. (*Moving to* CECILY.) Their explanations appear to be quite satisfactory, especially Mr. Worthing's. That seems to me to have the stamp of truth upon it.

CECILY. I am more than content with what Mr. Moncrieff said. His voice alone inspires one with absolute credulity.

GWENDOLEN. Then you think we should forgive them?

CECILY. Yes. I mean no.

GWENDOLEN. True! I had forgotten. There are principles at stake that one cannot surrender. Which of us should tell them? The task is not a pleasant one.

CECILY. Could we not both speak at the same time?

GWENDOLEN. An excellent idea! I nearly always speak at the same time as other people. Will you take the time from me?

CECILY. Certainly. (GWENDOLEN *beats time with uplifted finger.*)

GWENDOLEN *and* CECILY (*speaking together*). Your Christian names are still an insuperable barrier. That is all!

JACK *and* ALGERNON (*speaking together*). Our Christian names! Is that all? But we are going to be christened this afternoon.

GWENDOLEN (*to* JACK). For my sake you are prepared to do this terrible thing?

JACK. I am.

CECILY (*to* ALGERNON). To please me you are ready to face this fearful ordeal?

ALGERNON. I am!

GWENDOLEN. How absurd to talk of the equality of the sexes! Where questions of self-sacrifice are concerned, men are infinitely beyond us.

JACK. We are. (*Clasps hands with* ALGERNON.)

CECILY. They have moments of physical courage of which we women know absolutely nothing.

GWENDOLEN (*to* JACK). Darling!

ALGERNON (*to* CECILY). Darling! (*They fall into each other's arms.*)

(*Enter* MERRIMAN. *When he enters he coughs loudly, seeing the situation.*)

MERRIMAN. Ahem! Ahem! Lady Bracknell!

JACK. Good heavens!

(*Enter* LADY BRACKNELL. *The couples separate in alarm. Exit* MERRIMAN.)

LADY BRACKNELL. Gwendolen! What does this mean?

GWENDOLEN. Merely that I am engaged to be married to Mr. Worthing, Mamma.

LADY BRACKNELL. Come here. Sit down. Sit down immediately. Hesitation of any kind is a sign of mental decay in the young, of physical weakness in the old. (*Turns to* JACK.) Apprised, sir, of my daughter's sudden flight by her trusty maid, whose confidence I purchased by means of a small coin, I followed her at once by a luggage train. Her unhappy father is, I am glad to say, under the impression that she is attending a more than usually lengthy lecture by the University Extension Scheme on the Influence of a Permanent Income on Thought. I do not propose to undeceive him. Indeed I have never undeceived him on any question. I would consider it wrong. But of course, you will clearly understand that all communication between yourself and my daughter must cease immediately from this moment. On this point, as indeed on all points, I am firm.

JACK. I am engaged to be married to Gwendolen, Lady Bracknell!

LADY BRACKNELL. You are nothing of the kind, sir. And now, as regards Algernon! . . . Algernon!

ALGERNON. Yes, Aunt Augusta.

LADY BRACKNELL. May I ask if it is in this house that your invalid friend Mr. Bunbury resides?

ALGERNON (*stammering*). Oh, no! Bunbury doesn't live here. Bunbury is somewhere else at present. In fact, Bunbury is dead.

LADY BRACKNELL. Dead! When did Mr. Bunbury die? His death must have been extremely sudden.

ALGERNON (*airily*). Oh, I killed Bunbury this afternoon. I mean poor Bunbury died this afternoon.

LADY BRACKNELL. What did he die of?

ALGERNON. Bunbury? Oh, he was quite exploded.

LADY BRACKNELL. Exploded! Was he the victim of a revolutionary outrage? I was not aware that Mr. Bunbury was interested in social legislation. If so, he is well punished for his morbidity.

ALGERNON. My dear Aunt Augusta, I mean he was found out! The doctors found out that Bunbury could not live, that is what I mean—so Bunbury died.

LADY BRACKNELL. He seems to have had great confidence in the opinion of his physicians. I am glad, however, that he made up his mind at the last to some definite course of action, and acted under proper medical advice. And now that we have finally got rid of this Mr. Bunbury, may I ask, Mr. Worthing, who is that young person whose hand my nephew Algernon is now holding in what seems to me a peculiarly unnecessary manner?

JACK. That lady is Miss Cecily Cardew, my ward. (LADY BRACKNELL *bows coldly to* CECILY.)

ALGERNON. I am engaged to be married to Cecily, Aunt Augusta.

LADY BRACKNELL. I beg your pardon?

CECILY. Mr. Moncrieff and I are engaged to be married, Lady Bracknell.

LADY BRACKNELL (*with a shiver, crossing to the sofa and sitting down*). I do not know whether there is anything peculiarly exciting in the air of this particular part of Hertfordshire, but the number of engagements that go on seems to me considerably above the proper average that statistics have laid down for our guidance. I think some preliminary enquiry on my part would not be out of place. Mr. Worthing, is Miss Cardew at all connected with any of the larger railway stations in London? I merely desire information. Until yesterday I had no idea that there were any families or persons whose origin was a Terminus. (JACK *looks perfectly furious, but restrains himself.*)

JACK (*in a clear, cold voice*). Miss Cardew is the granddaughter of the late Mr. Thomas Cardew of 149, Belgrave Square, S.W.; Gervase Park, Dorking, Surrey; and the Sporran, Fifeshire, N. B.

LADY BRACKNELL. That sounds not unsatisfactory. Three addresses always inspire confidence, even in tradesmen. But what proof have I of their authenticity?

JACK. I have carefully preserved the Court Guide of the period. They are open to your inspection, Lady Bracknell.

LADY BRACKNELL (*grimly*). I have known strange errors in that publication.

JACK. Miss Cardew's family solicitors are Messrs. Markby, Markby, and Markby.

LADY BRACKNELL. Markby, Markby, and Markby? A firm of the very highest position in their profession. Indeed I am told that one of the Mr. Markbys is occasionally to be seen at dinner parties. So far I am satisfied.

JACK (*very irritably*). How extremely kind of you, Lady Bracknell! I have also in my possession, you will be pleased to hear, certificates of Miss Cardew's birth, baptism, whooping cough, registration, vaccination, confirmation, and the measles; both the German and the English variety.

LADY BRACKNELL. Ah! A life crowded with incident, I see; though perhaps somewhat too exciting for a young girl. I am not myself in favor of premature experiences. (*Rises, looks at her watch.*) Gwendolen! the time approaches for our departure. We have not a moment to lose. As a matter of form, Mr. Worthing, I had better ask you if Miss Cardew has any little fortune?

JACK. Oh, about a hundred and thirty thousand pounds in the Funds. That is all. Good-bye, Lady Bracknell. So pleased to have seen you.

LADY BRACKNELL (*sitting down again*). A moment, Mr. Worthing. A hundred and thirty thousand pounds! And in the Funds! Miss Cardew seems to me a most attractive young lady, now that I look at her. Few girls of the present day have any really solid qualities, any of the qualities that last, and improve with time. We live, I regret to say, in an age of surfaces. (*To* CECILY.) Come over here, dear. (CECILY *goes across.*) Pretty child! your dress is sadly simple, and your hair seems almost as Nature might have left it. But we can soon alter all that. A thoroughly experienced French maid produces a really marvellous result in a very brief space of time. I remember recommending one to young Lady Lancing, and after three months her own husband did not know her.

JACK (*aside*). And after six months nobody knew her.

LADY BRACKNELL (*glares at* JACK *for a few moments, then bends, with a practised smile, to* CECILY). Kindly turn round, sweet child. (CECILY *turns completely round.*) No, the side view is what I want. (CECILY *presents her profile.*) Yes, quite as I expected. There are distinct social possibilities in your profile. The two weak points in our age are its want of principle and its want of profile. The chin a little higher, dear. Style largely depends on the way the chin is worn. They are worn very high, just at present. Algernon!

ALGERNON. Yes, Aunt Augusta!

LADY BRACKNELL. There are distinct social possibilities in Miss Cardew's profile.

ALGERNON. Cecily is the sweetest, dearest, prettiest girl in the whole world. And I don't care twopence about social possibilities.

LADY BRACKNELL. Never speak disrespectfully of society, Algernon. Only people who can't get into it do that. (*To* CECILY.) Dear child, of course you know that Algernon has nothing but his debts to depend upon. But I do not approve of mercenary marriages. When I married Lord Bracknell I had no fortune of any kind. But I never dreamed for a moment of allowing that to stand in my way. Well, I suppose I must give my consent.

ALGERNON. Thank you, Aunt Augusta.

LADY BRACKNELL. Cecily, you may kiss me!

CECILY (*kisses her*). Thank you, Lady Bracknell.

LADY BRACKNELL. You may also address me as Aunt Augusta for the future.

CECILY. Thank you, Aunt Augusta.

LADY BRACKNELL. The marriage, I think, had better take place quite soon.

ALGERNON. Thank you, Aunt Augusta.

CECILY. Thank you, Aunt Augusta.

LADY BRACKNELL. To speak frankly, I am not in favour of long engagements. They give people the opportunity of finding out each other's character before marriage, which I think is never advisable.

JACK. I beg your pardon for interrupting you, Lady Bracknell, but this engagement is quite out of the question. I am Miss Cardew's guardian, and she cannot marry without my consent until she comes of age. That consent I absolutely decline to give.

LADY BRACKNELL. Upon what grounds, may I ask? Algernon is an extremely, I may almost say an ostentatiously, eligible young man. He has nothing, but he looks everything. What more can one desire?

JACK. It pains me very much to have to speak frankly to you, Lady Bracknell, about your nephew, but the fact is that I do not approve at all of his moral character. I suspect him of being untruthful. (ALGERNON *and* CECILY *look at him in indignant amazement.*)

LADY BRACKNELL. Untruthful! My nephew Algernon? Impossible! He is an Oxonian.

JACK. I fear there can be no possible doubt about the matter. This afternoon, during my temporary absence in London on an important question of romance, he obtained admission to my house by means of the false pretence of being my brother. Under an assumed name he drank, I've just been informed by my butler, an entire pint bottle of my Perrier-Jouet, Brut, '89; a wine I was specially reserving for myself. Continuing his disgraceful deception, he succeeded in the course of the afternoon in alienating the affections of my only ward. He subsequently stayed to tea, and devoured every single muffin. And what makes his conduct all the more heartless is that he was perfectly well aware from the first that I have no brother, that I never had a brother, and that I don't intend to have a brother, not even of any kind. I distinctly told him so myself yesterday afternoon.

LADY BRACKNELL. Ahem! Mr. Worthing, after careful

consideration I have decided entirely to overlook my nephew's conduct to you.

JACK. That is very generous of you, Lady Bracknell. My own decision, however, is unalterable. I decline to give my consent.

LADY BRACKNELL (*to* CECILY). Come here, sweet child. (CECILY *goes over.*) How old are you, dear?

CECILY. Well, I am really only eighteen, but I always admit to twenty when I go to evening parties.

LADY BRACKNELL. You are perfectly right in making some slight alteration. Indeed, no woman should ever be quite accurate about her age. It looks so calculating. . . . (*In meditative manner.*) Eighteen, but admitting to twenty at evening parties. Well, it will not be very long before you are of age and free from the restraints of tutelage. So I don't think your guardian's consent is, after all, a matter of any importance.

JACK. Pray excuse me, Lady Bracknell, for interrupting you again, but it is only fair to tell you that according to the terms of her grandfather's will Miss Cardew does not come legally of age till she is thirty-five.

LADY BRACKNELL. That does not seem to me to be a grave objection. Thirty-five is a very attractive age. London society is full of women of the very highest birth who have, of their own free choice, remained thirty-five for years. Lady Dumbleton is an instance in point. To my own knowledge she has been thirty-five ever since she arrived at the age of forty, which was many years ago now. I see no reason why our dear Cecily should not be even still more attractive at the age you mention than she is at present. There will be a large accumulation of property.

CECILY. Algy, could you wait for me till I was thirty-five?

ALGERNON. Of course I could, Cecily. You know I could.

CECILY. Yes, I felt it instinctively, but I couldn't wait

all that time. I hate waiting even five minutes for any-body. It always makes me rather cross. I am not punctual myself, I know, but I do like punctuality in others, and waiting, even to be married, is quite out of the question.

ALGERNON. Then what is to be done, Cecily?

CECILY. I don't know, Mr. Moncrieff.

LADY BRACKNELL. My dear Mr. Worthing, as Miss Cardew states positively that she cannot wait till she is thirty-five—a remark which I am bound to say seems to me to show a somewhat impatient nature—I would beg of you to reconsider your decision.

JACK. But my dear Lady Bracknell, the matter is en-tirely in your own hands. The moment you consent to my marriage with Gwendolen, I will most gladly allow your nephew to form an alliance with my ward.

LADY BRACKNELL (*rising and drawing herself up*). You must be quite aware that what you propose is out of the question.

JACK. Then a passionate celibacy is all that any of us can look forward to.

LADY BRACKNELL. That is not the destiny I propose for Gwendolen. Algernon, of course, can choose for himself. (*Pulls out her watch.*) Come, dear, (GWENDO-LEN *rises*) we have already missed five, if not six, trains. To miss any more might expose us to comment on the platform.

(*Enter* DR. CHASUBLE.)

CHASUBLE. Everything is quite ready for the christenings.

LADY BRACKNELL. The christenings, sir! Is not that somewhat premature?

CHASUBLE (*looking rather puzzled, and pointing to* JACK *and* ALGERNON). Both these gentlemen have ex-pressed a desire for immediate baptism.

LADY BRACKNELL. At their age? The idea is grotesque

and irreligious! Algernon, I forbid you to be baptised. I will not hear of such excesses. Lord Bracknell would be highly displeased if he learned that that was the way in which you wasted your time and money.

CHASUBLE. Am I to understand then that there are to be no christenings at all this afternoon?

JACK. I don't think that, as things are now, it would be of much practical value to either of us, Dr. Chasuble.

CHASUBLE. I am grieved to hear such sentiments from you, Mr. Worthing. They savour of the heretical views of the Anabaptists, views that I have completely refuted in four of my unpublished sermons. However, as your present mood seems to be one peculiarly secular, I will return to the church at once. Indeed, I have just been informed by the pew-opener that for the last hour and a half Miss Prism has been waiting for me in the vestry.

LADY BRACKNELL (*starting*). Miss Prism! Did I hear you mention a Miss Prism?

CHASUBLE. Yes, Lady Bracknell. I am on my way to join her.

LADY BRACKNELL. Pray allow me to detain you for a moment. This matter may prove to be one of vital importance to Lord Bracknell and myself. Is this Miss Prism a female of repellent aspect, remotely connected with education?

CHASUBLE (*somewhat indignantly*). She is the most cultivated of ladies, and the very picture of respectability.

LADY BRACKNELL. It is obviously the same person. May I ask what position she holds in your household?

CHASUBLE (*severely*). I am a celibate, madam.

JACK (*interposing*). Miss Prism, Lady Bracknell, has been for the last three years Miss Cardew's esteemed governesss and valued companion.

LADY BRACKNELL. In spite of what I hear of her, I must see her at once. Let her be sent for.

CHASUBLE (*looking off*). She approaches; she is nigh.

(*Enter* MISS PRISM *hurriedly.*)

MISS PRISM. I was told you expected me in the vestry, dear Canon. I have been waiting for you there for an hour and three-quarters. (*Catches sight of* LADY BRACKNELL, *who has fixed her with a stony glare.* MISS PRISM *grows pale and quails. She looks anxiously round as if desirous to escape.*)

LADY BRACKNELL (*in a severe, judicial voice*). Prism! (MISS PRISM *bows her head in shame.*) Come here, Prism! (MISS PRISM *approaches in a humble manner.*) Where is that baby? (*General consternation. The Canon starts back in horror.* ALGERNON *and* JACK *pretend to be anxious to shield* CECILY *and* GWENDOLEN *from hearing the details of a terrible public scandal.*) Twenty-eight years ago, Prism, you left Lord Bracknell's house, Number 104, Upper Grosvenor Street, in charge of a perambulator that contained a baby, of the male sex. You never returned. A few weeks later, through the elaborate investigations of the Metropolitan police, the perambulator was discovered at midnight, standing by itself in a remote corner of Bayswater. It contained the manuscript of a three-volume novel of more than usually revolting sentimentality. (MISS PRISM *starts in involuntary indignation.*) But the baby was not there! (*Everyone looks at* MISS PRISM.) Prism, where is that baby? (*A pause.*)

MISS PRISM. Lady Bracknell, I admit with shame that I do not know. I only wish I did. The plain facts of the case are these. On the morning of the day you mention, a day that is forever branded on my memory, I prepared as usual to take the baby out in its perambulator. I had also with me a somewhat old but capacious hand-bag in which I had intended to place the manuscript of a work of fiction that I had written during my few unoccupied hours. In a moment of mental abstraction, for which I never can forgive myself, I deposited the manuscript in the bassinette, and placed the baby in the hand-bag.

JACK (*who had been listening attentively*). But where did you deposit the hand-bag?

MISS PRISM. Do not ask me, Mr. Worthing.

JACK. Miss Prism, this is a matter of no small importance to me. I insist on knowing where you deposited the hand-bag that contained that infant.

MISS PRISM. I left it in the cloak-room of one of the larger railway stations in London.

JACK. What railway station?

MISS PRISM (*quite crushed*). Victoria. The Brighton line. (*Sinks into a chair.*)

JACK. I must retire to my room for a moment. Gwendolen, wait here for me.

GWENDOLEN. If you are not too long, I will wait here for you all my life.

(*Exit* JACK *in great excitement.*)

CHASUBLE. What do you think this means, Lady Bracknell?

LADY BRACKNELL. I dare not even suspect, Dr. Chasuble. I need hardly tell you that in families of high position strange coincidences are not supposed to occur. They are hardly considered the thing. (*Noises heard overhead as if someone was throwing trunks about. Everybody looks up.*)

CECILY. Uncle Jack seems strangely agitated.

CHASUBLE. Your guardian has a very emotional nature.

LADY BRACKNELL. This noise is extremely unpleasant. It sounds as if he was having an argument. I dislike arguments of any kind. They are always vulgar, and often convincing.

CHASUBLE (*looking up*). It has stopped now. (*The noise is redoubled.*)

LADY BRACKNELL. I wish he would arrive at some conclusion.

GWENDOLEN. The suspense is terrible. I hope it will last.

(*Enter* JACK *with a hand-bag of black leather in his hand.*)

JACK (*rushing over to* MISS PRISM). Is this the hand-bag, Miss Prism? Examine it carefully before you speak. The happiness of more than one life depends on your answer.

MISS PRISM (*calmly*). It seems to be mine. Yes, here is the injury it received through the upsetting of a Gower Street omnibus in younger and happier days. Here is the stain on the lining caused by the explosion of a temperance beverage, an incident that occurred at Leamington. And here, on the lock, are my initials. I had forgotten that in an extravagant mood I had had them placed there. The bag is undoubtedly mine. I am delighted to have it so unexpectedly restored to me. It has been a great inconvenience being without it all these years.

JACK (*in a pathetic voice*). Miss Prism, more is restored to you than this hand-bag. I was the baby you placed in it.

MISS PRISM (*amazed*). You?

JACK (*embracing her*). Yes ... Mother!

MISS PRISM (*recoiling in indignant astonishment*). Mr. Worthing! I am unmarried!

JACK. Unmarried! I do not deny that is a serious blow. But after all, who has the right to cast a stone against one who has suffered? Cannot repentance wipe out an act of folly? Why should there be one law for men and another for women? Mother, I forgive you. (*Tries to embrace her again.*)

MISS PRISM (*still more indignant*). Mr. Worthing, there is some error. (*Pointing to* LADY BRACKNELL.) There is the lady who can tell you who you really are.

JACK (*after a pause*). Lady Bracknell, I hate to seem inquisitive, but would you kindly inform me who I am?

LADY BRACKNELL. I am afraid that the news I have to give you will not altogether please you. You are the son of my poor sister, Mrs. Moncrieff, and consequently Algernon's elder brother.

JACK. Algy's elder brother! Then I have a brother after all. I knew I had a brother! I always said I had a brother! Cecily, how could you have ever doubted that I had a brother? (*Seizes hold of* ALGERNON.) Dr. Chasuble, my unfortunate brother. Miss Prism, my unfortunate brother. Gwendolen, my unfortunate brother. Algy, you young scoundrel, you will have to treat me with more respect in the future. You have never behaved to me like a brother in all your life.

ALGERNON. Well, not till to-day, old boy, I admit. I did my best, however, though I was out of practice. (*Shakes hands.*)

GWENDOLEN (*to* JACK). My own! But what own are you? What is your Christian name, now that you have become someone else?

JACK. Good heavens! . . . I had quite forgotten that point. Your decision on the subject of my name is irrevocable, I suppose?

GWENDOLEN. I never change, except in my affections.

CECILY. What a noble nature you have, Gwendolen!

JACK. Then the question had better be cleared up at once. Aunt Augusta, a moment. At the time when Miss Prism left me in the hand-bag, had I been christened already?

LADY BRACKNELL. Every luxury that money could buy, including christening, had been lavished on you by your fond and doting parents.

JACK. Then I was christened! That is settled. Now, what name was I given? Let me know the worst.

LADY BRACKNELL. Being the eldest son you were naturally christened after your father.

JACK (*irritably*). Yes, but what was my father's Christian name?

LADY BRACKNELL (*meditatively*). I cannot at the present moment recall what the General's Christian name was. But I have no doubt he had one. He was eccentric, I admit. But only in later years. And that was the result of the Indian climate, and marriage, and indigestion, and other things of that kind.

JACK. Algy! Can't you recollect what our father's Christian name was?

ALGERNON. My dear boy, we were never even on speaking terms. He died before I was a year old.

JACK. His name would appear in the Army Lists of the period, I suppose, Aunt Augusta?

LADY BRACKNELL. The General was essentially a man of peace, except in his domestic life. But I have no doubt his name would appear in any military directory.

JACK. The Army Lists of the last forty years are here. These delightful records should have been my constant study. (*Rushes to bookcase and tears the books out.*) M. Generals ... Mallham, Maxbohm, Magley, what ghastly names they have—Markby, Migsby, Mobbs, Moncrieff! Lieutenant 1840, Captain, Lieutenant-Colonel, Colonel, General 1869, Christian names, Ernest John. (*Puts book very quietly down and speaks quite calmly.*) I always told you, Gwendolen, my name was Ernest, didn't I? Well, it is Ernest after all, I mean it naturally is Ernest.

LADY BRACKNELL. Yes, I remember the General was called Ernest. I knew I had some particular reason for disliking the name.

GWENDOLEN. Ernest! My own Ernest! I felt from the first that you could have no other name!

JACK. Gwendolen, it is a terrible thing for a man to find out suddenly that all his life he has been speaking nothing but the truth. Can you forgive me?

GWENDOLEN. I can. For I feel sure that you are sure to change.

JACK. My own one!

CHASUBLE (*to* MISS PRISM). Lætitia! (*Embraces her.*)

MISS PRISM (*enthusiastically*). Frederick! At last!

ALGERNON. Cecily! (*Embraces her.*) At last!

JACK. Gwendolen! (*Embraces her.*) At last!

LADY BRACKNELL. My nephew, you seem to be displaying signs of triviality.

JACK. On the contrary, Aunt Augusta, I've now realized for the first time in my life the vital Importance of Being Earnest.

TABLEAU

CURTAIN

Appendix

The Gribsby Episode
in The Importance of Being Earnest

The Introduction to this volume explains (page xxxi) that Wilde drafted *Earnest* in four acts and then revised it, at the producer's urging, into three acts. The final version is a far more polished work than is the four-act version, but we can regret the omission of what has come to be called the Gribsby Episode: A Mr. Gribsby, who is also a Mr. Parker, threatens to arrest Algernon, who is masquerading as Ernest Worthing, for debts that John incurred under the name of the imaginary Ernest. The manuscript is in the Arents Collection in the New York Public Library; we reproduce the episode with the library's permission. If the passage were to be inserted into the three-act version, it would belong on page 145–46, beginning when Merriman enters to say that he has unpacked Ernest's luggage.

THE GRIBSBY EPISODE

Enter MERRIMAN.

MERRIMAN. I have put Mr. Ernest's things in the room next to yours, sir. I suppose that is all right?

JACK. What?

MERRIMAN. Mr. Ernest's luggage, sir. I have unpacked it and I have put it in the room next to your own.

ALGERNON. I am afraid I can't stay more than a week, Jack, this time.

CECILY. A week? Will you really be able to stay over Monday?

ALGERNON. I think I can manage to stop over Monday, now.

CECILY. I am so glad.

MERRIMAN (*to* ERNEST). I beg your pardon, sir, there is an elderly gentleman wishes to see you. He has just come in a cab from the station. (*Hands card on salver.*)

ALGERNON. To see me?

MERRIMAN. Yes, sir.

ALGERNON (*reads card*). "Parker and Gribsby, Solicitors." I don't know anything about them. Who are they?

JACK (*takes card*). Parker and Gribsby. I wonder who they can be. I expect, Ernest, they have come about some business for your friend Bunbury. Perhaps Bunbury wants to make his will, and wishes you to be executor. (*To* MERRIMAN.) Show Messrs. Parker and Gribsby in at once.

MERRIMAN. There is only one gentleman in the hall, sir.

JACK. Show either Mr. Parker or Mr. Gribsby in.

MERRIMAN. Yes, sir.

Exit MERRIMAN.

JACK. I hope, Ernest, that I may rely on the statement you made to me last week when I finally settled all your bills for you. I hope you have no outstanding accounts of any kind.

ALGERNON. I haven't any debts at all, dear Jack. Thanks to your generosity I don't owe a penny, except for a few neckties, I believe.

JACK. I am sincerely glad to hear it.

MERRIMAN. Mr. Gribsby.

Enter GRIBSBY.

GRIBSBY (*to* CANON CHASUBLE). Mr. Ernest Worthing?

MISS PRISM. This is Mr. Ernest Worthing.

GRIBSBY. Mr. Ernest Worthing?

ALGERNON. Yes.

GRIBSBY. Of B 4, The Albany?

ALGERNON. Yes, that is my address.

GRIBSBY. I am very sorry, Mr. Worthing, but we have a writ of attachment for 20 days against you at the suit of the Savoy Hotel Co. Limited for £762.14.2.

ALGERNON. What perfect nonsense! I never dine at the Savoy at my own expense. I always dine at Willis's. It is far more expensive. I don't owe a penny to the Savoy.

GRIBSBY. The writ is marked as having been [served] on you personally at the Albany on May the 27th. Judgment was given in default against you on the fifth of June. Since then we have written to you no less than thirteen times, without receiving any reply. In the interest of our clients we had no option but to obtain an order for committal of your person. But, no doubt, Mr. Worthing, you will be able to settle the account without any further unpleasantness. Seven and six should be added to the bill of costs for expense of the cab which was hired for your convenience in case of any necessity of removal, but that, I am sure, is a contingency that is not likely to occur.

ALGERNON. Removal! What on earth do you mean by removal? I haven't the smallest intention of going away. I am staying here for a week. I am staying with my brother. (*Points to* JACK.)

GRIBSBY (*to* JACK). Pleased to meet you, sir.

ALGERNON (*to* GRIBSBY). If you imagine I am going to town the moment I arrive you are extremely mistaken.

GRIBSBY. I am merely a solicitor myself. I do not employ personal violence of any kind. The officer of the court whose function it is to seize the person of the debtor is waiting in the fly outside. He has considerable experience in these matters. In the point of fact he has arrested in the course of his duties nearly all the younger sons of the aristocracy, as well as several eldest sons, besides of course a good many members of the House of Lords. His style and manner are considered extremely good. Indeed, he looks more like a betting man than a court official. That is why we always employ him. But no doubt you will prefer to pay the bill.

ALGERNON. Pay it? How on earth am I going to do that? You don't suppose I have got any money? How perfectly silly you are. No gentleman ever has any money.

GRIBSBY. My experience is that it is usually relatives who pay.

JACK. Kindly allow me to see this bill, Mr. Gribsby ... (*Turns over immense folio.*) ... £762.14.2 since last October.... I am bound to say I never saw such reckless extravagance in all my life. (*Hands it to* DR. CHASUBLE.)

MISS PRISM. 762 pounds for eating! How grossly materialistic! There can be little good in any young man who eats so much, and so often.

CHASUBLE. It certainly is a painful proof of the disgraceful luxury of the age. We are far away from Wordsworth's plain living and high thinking.

JACK. Now, Dr. Chasuble, do you consider that I am in any way called upon to pay this monstrous account for my brother?

CHASUBLE. I am bound to say that I do not think so. It would be encouraging his profligacy.

MISS PRISM. As a man sows, so let him reap. This proposed incarceration might be most salutary. It is to be regretted that [it] is only for 20 days.

JACK. I am quite of your opinion.

ALGERNON. My dear fellow, how ridiculous you are! You know perfectly well that the bill is really yours.

JACK. Mine?

ALGERNON. Yes, you know it is.

CHASUBLE. Mr. Worthing, if this is a jest, it is out of place.

MISS PRISM. It is gross effrontery. Just what I expected from him.

CECILY. It is ingratitude. I didn't expect that.

JACK. Never mind what he says. This is the way he always goes on. You mean now to say that you are not Ernest Worthing, residing at B 4, The Albany? I wonder, as you are at it, that you don't deny being my brother at all. Why don't you?

ALGERNON. Oh! I am not going to do that, my dear fellow; it would be absurd. Of course, I'm your brother. And that is why you should pay this bill for me. What is the use of having a brother, if he doesn't pay one's bills for one?

JACK. Personally, if you ask me, I don't see any use in having a brother. As for paying your bill, I have not the smallest intention of doing anything of the kind. Dr. Chasuble, the worthy Rector of this parish, and Miss Prism, in whose admirable and sound judgment I place great reliance, are both of opinion that incarceration would do you a great deal of good. And I think so, too.

GRIBSBY (*pulls out watch*). I am sorry to disturb this pleasant family meeting, but time presses. We have to be at Holloway not later than four o'clock; otherwise it is difficult to obtain admission. The rules are very strict.

ALGERNON. Holloway!

GRIBSBY. It is at Holloway that detentions of this character take place always.

ALGERNON. Well, I really am not going to be imprisoned in the suburbs for having dined in the West End. It is perfectly ridiculous.

GRIBSBY. The bill is for suppers, not for dinners.

ALGERNON. I really don't care. All I say is that I am not going to be imprisoned in the suburbs.

GRIBSBY. The surroundings, I admit, are middle class;

but the gaol itself is fashionable and well-aired, and there are ample opportunities for taking exercise at certain stated hours of the day. In the case of a medical certificate, which is always easy to obtain, the hours can be extended.

ALGERNON. Exercise! Good God! No gentleman ever takes exercise. You don't seem to understand what a gentleman is.

GRIBSBY. I have met so many of them, sir, that I am afraid I don't. There are the most curious varieties of them. The result of cultivation, no doubt. Will you kindly come now, sir, if it will not be inconvenient to you.

ALGERNON (*appealingly*). Jack!

MISS PRISM. Pray be firm, Mr. Worthing.

CHASUBLE. This is an occasion on which any weakness would be out of place. It would be a form of self-deception.

JACK. I am quite firm; and I don't know what weakness or deception of any kind is.

CECILY. Uncle Jack! I think you have a little money of mine, haven't you? Let me pay this bill. I wouldn't like your own brother to be in prison.

JACK. Oh, you can't pay it, Cecily, that is nonsense.

CECILY. Then you will, won't you? I think you would be sorry if you thought your own brother was shut up. Of course, I am quite disappointed with him.

JACK. You won't speak to him again, Cecily, will you?

CECILY. Certainly not, unless, of course, he speaks to me first; it would be very rude not to answer him.

JACK. Well, I'll take care he doesn't speak to you. I'll take care he doesn't speak to anybody in this house. The man should be cut. Mr. Gribsby—

GRIBSBY. Yes, sir.

JACK. I'll pay this bill for my brother. It is the last bill I shall ever pay for him, too. How much is it?

GRIBSBY. £762.14.2. May I ask your full name, sir?

JACK. Mr. John Worthing J.P., The Manor House, Woolton. Does that satisfy you?

GRIBSBY. Oh, certainly, sir, certainly! It was a mere formality. (*To* MISS PRISM.) Handsome place. Ah! the cab will be 5/9 extra—hired for the convenience of the client.

JACK. All right.

MISS PRISM. I must say that I think such generosity quite foolish. Especially paying the cab.

CHASUBLE (*with a wave of the hand*). The heart has its wisdom as well as the head, Miss Prism.

JACK. Payable to Gribsby and Parker, I suppose.

GRIBSBY. Yes, sir. Kindly don't cross the cheque. Thank you.

JACK. You are Gribsby, aren't you? What is Parker like?

GRIBSBY. I am both, sir. Gribsby when I am on unpleasant business, Parker on occasions of a less serious kind.

JACK. The next time I see you I hope you will be Parker.

GRIBSBY. I hope so, sir. (*To* DR. CHASUBLE.) Good day. (DR. CHASUBLE *bows coldly.*) Good day. (MISS PRISM *bows coldly.*) Hope I shall have the pleasure of meeting you again. (*To* ALGERNON.)

ALGERNON. I sincerely hope not. What ideas you have of the sort of society a gentleman wants to mix in. No gentleman ever wants to know a solicitor who wants to imprison one in the suburbs.

GRIBSBY. Quite so, quite so.

ALGERNON. By the way, Gribsby. Gribsby, you are not to go back to the station in that cab. That is my cab. It was taken for my convenience. You and the gentleman who looks like the betting man have got to walk to the station. And a very good thing, too. Solicitors don't walk nearly enough. They bolt. But they don't walk. I don't know any solicitor who takes sufficient exercise. As a rule they sit in stuffy offices all day long neglecting their business.

JACK. You can take the cab, Mr. Gribsby.

GRIBSBY. Thank you, sir.

Exit GRIBSBY.

ALGERNON. Well, I must say that I think you might have let me play my joke on Gribsby. It was rather a good joke in its way. And of course I wasn't serious about it.

Afterword

We both first read Oscar Wilde while taking college courses in British literature. Coming between the novels of George Eliot and Thomas Hardy or after the works of Alfred Tennyson, Matthew Arnold, Walter Pater, and George Bernard Shaw, Wilde usually appeared around the middle of the semester, a breath of fresh air amidst the smoke and gloom of Victorian seriousness. His writing sparkled; one laughed out loud while reading him. *Lady Windermere's Fan* was consumed on a sunny afternoon early in a warm spring break. A stroll to a local bookstore yielded a secondhand copy of Wilde's *Works* and further pleasures: the bon mots of Lord Henry Wotton in *The Picture of Dorian Gray*; the epigrammatic repartee of Lady Bracknell and Jack Worthing in *The Importance of Being Earnest*; the biting ironies of "The Ballad of Reading Gaol"; and the outrageous banter of Cyril and Vivian in "The Decay of Lying." Writing brilliantly in every genre in spite of a relatively short career, Wilde strongly recalls another Irish writer, Oliver Goldsmith, whose works also sometimes seem to stand apart from his age, inhabiting a sunny island of their own making.

We returned to Wilde a decade later through a play by Moisés Kaufman called *Gross Indecency: The Three Trials of Oscar Wilde*, which played to sellout houses in New York during the 1997–98 theater season. Many readers will better know Kaufman as the author of *The Laramie Project* (2001), about the murder of Matthew Shepard, one of the most infamous hate crimes of the 1990s. In its short life it has already become one of the most performed plays of the twenty-first century; its popularity among student and community theater groups has stemmed from its progressive social politics, its simple yet experimental stage practice, and its ability to offer a large number of roles to actors of both sexes and all ages. At the time we first saw it, *Gross Indecency* offered similar pleasures, but through a smaller, entirely male cast. Drawn almost exclusively from the transcripts of Wilde's three trials and from reviews and commentary about them, the play is remarkably hard-hitting. It grips audiences through its ability to portray Wilde's downfall through an unfolding chain of events narrated by several voices. Throughout *Gross Indecency*, Kaufman portrays Wilde sympathetically and in his own words; at the same time, he shows us the degree to which Wilde participated in his own legal suicide by initiating the criminal prosecution that eventually resulted in his own arrest and imprisonment and, as the case unfolded, by lying to his attorney about his sexual practices and history. He stands in the play at once as the victim of social intolerance and as a political target whose aestheticism posed a revolutionary threat to Victorian moral and artistic conventions. And in both roles, he is more than credible.

At the time of the first trial in 1895, Wilde had two hit plays on London's West End: *An Ideal Husband* and *The Importance of Being Earnest*. He was also in the midst of an affair with Lord Alfred Douglas, whose father, the Marquess of Queensberry, disapproved of his son's association with Wilde. Queensberry had been feuding with his son for years, and the feud reached its height when Douglas refused to break off the relationship. At this point, the Marquess began a campaign of escalating threats and stunts toward Wilde, culminating in his leaving a calling card at Wilde's club on which he had written, "Oscar Wilde posing somdomite" (*sic*). At Douglas's urging, Wilde brought a prosecution against Queensberry for criminal libel for publishing such a statement; Queensberry's legal defense was that the statement was true and was made for the public benefit. In so doing, he also alleged that Wilde had published two immoral works: *The Picture of Dorian Gray*, published in 1891, and "Phrases and Philosophies for the Use of the Young," which had been published in an Oxford undergraduate literary magazine, *The Chameleon*, alongside poems by Douglas and other writers celebrating same-sex love. During the proceedings of the first trial, Wilde thus found himself being cross-examined not only about his own published works and aesthetic philosophy, but also about Douglas's writings and editorial choices. In defending Queensberry against Wilde's charges of criminal libel, the lawyers for the defense sought to show through Wilde's writings—as well as through testimony concerning Wilde's relations with other young men—that Wilde was indeed "posing" as a "sodomite," or homosexual. Their aim, in other words, was to insist that the jury *equate* the life and the published work, and, this equation made, to declare Queensberry's statement both true and for the public benefit.

This is a remarkable connection on which to insist. Anyone who has written a story, poem, or play that places characters of different opinions in conflict with one another will acknowledge the narrowness of such an aesthetic vision. One of the cautions students regularly receive is never to conflate writer and work. Authors, after all, create fictional universes, and these worlds are inhabited by characters, pronouncements, moods, and arguments that bear no necessary relation to the author's own views. Yet, at the same time, we recognize how often, as readers, we have yielded to this very temptation—how, when reading a particularly interesting work, we begin speculating as to which parts reflect the author's actual beliefs.

Wilde invited, and continues to invite, such conjectures—in part because his fame made him a popular object of rumor and gossip, and in part because, like Byron, his writings contained figures that seemed to mirror his public persona. This is especially true of Wilde's plays. There, the characters deliver urbane one-liners similar to those Wilde tossed off in real life. Asked whether he had anything to declare on arriving to America, Wilde famously responded, "I have nothing to declare but my genius"; reprimanded for flattering Lady Windermere unnecessarily, Lord Darlington similarly quips, "I can resist everything but temptation" (*Lady Windermere's Fan*, page 44). When faced with characters who speak like Wilde and who (in some productions) were cast even to look like him, it is hard to believe the resemblance merely accidental. Wilde, moreover, repeatedly cultivated just this sort of coincidence between his work and his life, so much so that Queensberry's lawyer, Edward Carson—ironically, a former college classmate and friend of Wilde's—succeeded in making the association stick in a court of law.

This history acknowledged, we nevertheless invite readers to consider a broader context, one that acknowledges the importance of Wilde's biography without rendering his works subject to it. Rather than reading Wilde's plays merely as keys to the life of the author, we might begin by noticing how different the plays are from one another. *Salomé* may treat subjects similar to those invoked in *Lady Windermere's Fan*—the emotional violence of desire and the costs of transgressing social boundaries, to name two—but it does so without sentimentality and to different ends. And while the dialogue of *The Importance of Being Earnest* may recall the witticisms of *Lady Windermere's Fan*, the former play celebrates the pursuit of pleasure, while the latter condemns it. At the very least, *Salomé*, *Lady Windermere's Fan*, and *The Importance of Being Earnest* provide us contrasting glimpses of Wilde through a range of genres: the first is lyrical and tragic; the second is comic and melodramatic by turns; the third is outrageously artificial and satirical. Each aims not only to pillory moral sensibilities but also to challenge expectations regarding what a given dramatic mode can and should accomplish.

As the Introduction to this edition notes, *Salomé* was refused a license to be performed in England because it violated long-standing prohibitions on the depiction of biblical characters. That fact alone would be enough to make *Salomé* a noteworthy play; it also provides us, though, with a means of understanding Wilde's particular brand of subversion. Rather than take up the parable of John the Baptist's death as a vehicle for moral instruction, *Salomé* contrasts the purity of the Bible's language with the amoral nature of some of its characters. In this way, the play adapts sacred language to further the claims of Art. Its most important scenes from a dramatic standpoint are therefore also the most poetic. Tricked by his own lust into promising Salomé anything she desires, Herod begs her not to request the head of Jokanaan, and his desperation yields a stream of beautiful images: "sapphires big like eggs," "wondrous turquoises," and, in a burst of geological lyricism, "chrysolites and beryls and chrysoprases and rubies [. . .] sardonyx and hyacinth stones, and stones of chalcedony" (pages 32–33), all of which fire the imagination and also leave us wondering (in all likelihood) what some of these wonderful-sounding stones are.

Yet the play also depicts an atmosphere of strict cultural mores in which any kind of difference—whether religious or sexual, social or racial—is declared to be "terrible," "ridiculous," and "impossible to understand" (5–6), as this opening exchange between one of the soldiers and the Cappadocian demonstrates:

FIRST SOLDIER. The Jews worship a God that one cannot see.

THE CAPPADOCIAN. I cannot understand that.

FIRST SOLDIER. In fact, they only believe in things that one cannot see.

THE CAPPADOCIAN. That seems to me altogether ridiculous.   (page 5)

At this moment, we first hear the voice of Jokanaan. Not surprisingly, his prophecies produce either incomprehension or demands that he be silenced. Of course, the most overt challenge *Salomé* poses to its readers, then and now, is sexual. Exemplified by Herod's incestuous desire for Salomé and Salomé's masochistic desire for Jokanaan, these taboos are portrayed in the same terms of repression that characterize the play's cultural setting. On first hearing the voice of Jokanaan, Salomé thus adopts the uncomprehending language used by the soldiers when confronted with anything different from themselves. Having heard from others that Jokanaan says "terrible things," Salomé's first assessment of him is to declare, "Ah, but he is terrible, he is terrible!" (page 11). Within the narrow horizons of understanding established in the first pages of the play, prophets cannot be understood, friendships cannot be valued, and moral prohibitions cannot be maintained. Constantly urged by his wife not to look on her daughter, Herod cannot help but desire Salomé; by the play's same unsavory logic, Salomé's forbidden lust for Jokanaan only becomes more intense amidst the Young Syrian's urgings that she return to the banquet.

Wilde offers less extreme visions of convention in *Lady Windermere's Fan* and *The Importance of Being Earnest*: neither play disciplines female transgression with death, let alone foretells religious apocalypse. Of the two comedies, *Lady Windermere* more closely resembles *Salomé* in its insistence on melodrama and the maintenance of social standards. Mrs. Erlynne may not forfeit her life as punishment for leaving her husband, but she does pay for her sin by surrendering her rights as a mother and losing her social respectability. Moreover, the play continually makes clear the difficulties involved in regaining either of these things. She schemes incessantly, even resorting to blackmail, and must remarry to secure her social position.

As if anticipating her new status, Mrs. Erlynne insists that her husband-to-be, Lord Augustus Lorton, cease to drink or play cards. Her reasons, however, are different from those of maintaining respectability. A central irony of *Lady Windermere's Fan* is that the social policing of female reputation is enforced primarily by men, who assemble over cards or alcohol to pass judgment on the Lady Windermeres and Mrs. Erlynnes of the world. In asking Lord Augustus to change his behavior, Mrs. Erlynne actually wants to remove him from these all-male cabals and, in the process, cease the repressive habits they perpetuate. She even asks him to leave England after their marriage (as if England were a massive allmale club), and Lord Augustus, in a surprising display of open-mindedness and affection in a play that often lacks both of these things, accedes.

One of the unintentional lessons we might take from *Lady Windermere's Fan* is that every happy marriage is preserved through deception. Certainly this is the case with Lord and Lady Windermere, but it also extends to the other pairs in the play, especially the Duke and Duchess of Berwick and (in another kind of relationship) the Duchess of Berwick and her daughter, Agatha, who never openly acknowledge the mercenary nature of matchmaking among the elite. Deception is at the heart of *The Importance of Being Earnest* as well, but with more pleasant consequences. Wilde's most famous play depicts the machinations of two characters, Algernon and Jack, whose respectability depends on their con-

structing alternate identities for themselves. Algernon's
fictitious friend, Bunbury, serves both as a synonym for
one who lies (a Bunburyist) and for lying (Bunburying) itself, while Jack's alter ego, Ernest Worthing, is so
central to the plot as to give the play its title and final
line. After mutual attempts to repudiate their alter egos
and marry the women they love, with varying degrees of
farce (both men squabble about being rechristened Ernest, for example), the pair finally reaches a moment in
which they can justify their marriage proposals to Lady
Bracknell. At that moment, both men reject their alter
egos and take on actual identities: Algernon announces
that Bunbury has "quite exploded," while Jack learns
that he is Algernon's older brother and indeed named
Ernest (pages 167, 177–79).

Even as the play heads toward a double marriage,
presumably based on Algernon's and Jack's true identities, the characters continue to affirm the necessity of
deceiving others, particularly one's spouse. In approv-
ing Algernon and Cecily's marriage, for example, Lady
Bracknell opines that she is "not in favour of long engagements. They give people the opportunity of finding out each other's character before marriage, which
I think is never advisable." (page 171). On the brink of
their marriage, Jack even apologizes to Gwendolen for
actually being named Ernest:

JACK. Gwendolen, it is a terrible thing for a man to
find out suddenly that all his life he has been speaking
nothing but the truth. Can you forgive me?

GWENDOLEN. I can. For I feel sure that you are sure
to change.

JACK. My own one! [. . .] Gwendolen! *(Embraces
her.)* At last!   (pages 179–80)

The device wielded here is structural irony, the sys-
tematic overturning of worn maxims to uncover even

deeper truths. In this case, beneath the clever banter of the lovers lies a fairly fundamental statement about the nature of creativity. Having long congratulated himself on his ability to create and sustain an entirely fictional existence—not unlike the old fraternity trick of creating a fictitious student, enrolling him for classes, and fooling the powers that be into giving him a degree—Jack finds that he has been merely truthful, which means his actions show no creativity at all. Gwendolen, meanwhile, assures Jack of her continuing faith in his imaginative genius; their embrace affirms that their marriage will thrive on as yet unimagined deceptions.

In many ways, we can read *The Importance of Being Earnest* as a mirror for Wilde's own double life, which alternately fueled his popular mystique and his emotional needs. For Algernon and Jack, successfully maintaining an alternate existence, however artificially or farcically, affirms one's superior intelligence and provides an escape from repressive social codes. This insistence is perhaps the most radical aspect of Wilde's "trivial comedy for serious people," even if Wilde himself could not achieve it in his own life.

—Elise Bruhl and Michael Gamer

Suggested References

WILDE'S WRITINGS

The fourteen volumes of *Oscar Wilde: The Collected Edition*, ed. Robert Ross (1908) are not complete and they are not annotated, but they do include almost everything of importance that Wilde wrote except his letters. For the letters, see *Complete Letters of Oscar Wilde*, eds. Merlin Holland and Rupert Hart-Davis (2001). *Complete Works of Oscar Wilde*, intro. Merlin Holland (1994) is useful, though one looks forward to a new scholarly edition, *The Complete Works of Oscar Wilde*, general eds. Russell Jackson and Ian Small (2000–), of which at this time (spring 2011) only four volumes have been published—none of which includes any of the plays. Elsewhere there are, however, excellent editions of the comedies: *An Ideal Husband*, ed. Russell Jackson, 2nd ed. (1993); *The Importance of Being Earnest*, ed. Russell Jackson (1980); *Oscar Wilde's The Importance of Being Earnest: A Reconstructive Critical Edition of the Text of the First Production*, eds. Joseph Donohue and Ruth Berggren (1995); *Lady Windermere's Fan*, ed. Ian Small, 2nd ed. (1999); *A Woman of No Importance*, ed. Ian Small, 2nd ed. (1993). There are two useful collections of Wilde's critical writings: *Literary Criticism of Oscar Wilde*, ed. Stanley Weintraub (1968) and *The Artist as Critic: Critical Writings of Oscar Wilde*, ed. Richard Ellmann (1969).

REFERENCE WORKS

Karl Beckson, *The Oscar Wilde Encyclopedia* (1995); Ian Small, *Oscar Wilde Revalued: An Essay on New Materials of Research* (1993) identifies and describes manuscripts, comments on recent criticism, and ends with a bibliography of several hundred items; Ian Small, *Oscar Wilde: A Supplement to Oscar Wilde Revalued* (2000) similarly lists and evaluates material, from 1992 (the cutoff date for the previous volume) to 1999, but it also includes some early items that Small's earlier book inadvertently omitted.

BIOGRAPHIES AND CRITICAL STUDIES

Richard Ellmann's *Oscar Wilde* (1987) is a balanced scholarly account, though because Ellmann was dying when the book was in its final stages, it is marred by numerous errors. The 1988 American edition include some corrections, but for many additional corrections see Horst Schroeder, *Additions and Corrections to Richard Ellmann's Oscar* Wilde, 2nd ed. (2002). A good short introduction is John Sloan, *Oscar Wilde* (2003). Another useful general account is *The Cambridge Companion to Oscar Wilde*, ed. Peter Raby (1997), which includes fifteen essays by diverse hands, on a wide range of topics (Wilde the poet, Wilde the critic, Wilde on the stage, etc.). Books written from more specialized points of view include several that emphasize the gay Wilde: Ed Cohen, *Talk on the Wilde Side: Toward a Genealogy of Discourse on Male Sexualities* (1993); Gary Schmidgall, *The Stranger Wilde* (1994); and an especially balanced account of this topic, Alan Sinfield, *The Wilde Century: Effeminacy, Oscar Wilde and the Queer Moment* (1994).

For an examination of the writings of some forty critics at the end of the twentieth century, arranged by school of criticism (e.g., "Theater History," "Gay, Queer, and Gender Criticism," "Irish Ethnic Studies"), see Melissa Knox, *Oscar Wilde in the 1990s: The Critic as Creator* (2001).

THE PLAYS ON THE STAGE

Karl Beckson, *The Critical Heritage* (1970) reprints most of the early reviews of all the works. Robert Tanitch, *Oscar Wilde on Stage and Screen* (1999) is valuable but it is not as complete as it may seem to be. *Modern Drama* 37 (1994), devoted to Wilde, includes interesting discussions of productions, for instance Joel H. Kaplan's "Staging Wilde's Society Plays: A Conversation with Philip Prowse," pp. 192–201. Kaplan also has a useful essay, "Wilde on the Stage," in *The Cambridge Companion to Oscar Wilde*, ed. Peter Raby (1997). For a thorough discussion of *Salomé* on the stage (including transformations into film and into Strauss's opera), see William Tydeman and Steven Price, *Wilde: Salomé* (1996).

ADDITIONAL CRITICAL STUDIES

Julia Prewitt Brown, *Cosmopolitan Criticism: Oscar Wilde's Philosophy of Art* (1997); Sos Eltis, *Revising Wilde: Society and Subversion in the Plays of Oscar Wilde* (1996); Kerry Powell, *Oscar Wilde and the Theatre of the 1890s* (1990); Neil Sammells, *Wilde Style: The Plays and Prose of Oscar Wilde* (2000); Katharine Worth, *Oscar Wilde* (1983). College teachers will find useful *Approaches to Teaching the Works of Oscar Wilde*, ed. Philip E. Smith II (2008), which includes six essays on the comedies, five on *Salomé*, and two on the criticism. For an anthology of criticism of Wilde's best-known play, see *The Importance of Being Earnest: Modern Critical Interpretations*, ed. Harold Bloom (1988). On Wilde as a critic, see Lawrence Danson, *Wilde's Intentions: The Artist in His Criticism* (1997).

Connect with Berkley Publishing Online!

For sneak peeks into the newest releases, news on all your favorite authors, book giveaways, and a central place to connect with fellow fans—

"Like" and follow Berkley Publishing!

facebook.com/BerkleyPub
twitter.com/BerkleyPub
instagram.com/BerkleyPub

Oscar Wilde (1854–1900) was born in Dublin, Ireland. He was an outstanding student of classics at Trinity College, and in 1874, he entered Magdalen College, Oxford, where he won the Newdigate Prize with his poem "Ravenna" (1878). An early leader of the Aesthetic Movement, which advanced the concept of "Art for Art's Sake," Wilde became a prominent personality in literary and social circles. His volume of fairy tales, *The Happy Prince and Other Tales* (1888), was followed by *The Picture of Dorian Gray* (1891) and *The House of Pomegranates* (1892). However, it was not until his play *Lady Windermere's Fan* (1892) was presented to the public that he became widely famous. *A Woman of No Importance* (1893) and *The Importance of Being Earnest* (1895) confirmed his stature as a dramatist. In 1895, in response to an accusation of homosexuality, which was then illegal, he sued the Marquess of Queensberry for libel; the marquess was acquitted, and Wilde was then tried and convicted of "gross indecency" and sentenced to two years' imprisonment with hard labor. Upon his release in 1897, he settled on the Continent, where he wrote his most powerful and enduring poem, *The Ballad of Reading Gaol* (1898).

Sylvan Barnet is a Professor Emeritus of English at Tufts University and general editor of the Signet Classics Shakespeare.

Elise Bruhl is a Deputy City Solicitor in the City of Philadelphia Law Department. She has authored and coauthored articles on topics such as contract law, pro se litigation, Emma Hamilton, and Angela Carter. She is currently at work on a book, *Losing Cases,* which chronicles well-known trials, including the trials of Oscar Wilde. **Michael Gamer** is Associate Professor of English at the University of Pennsylvania and author of *Romanticism and the Gothic: Genre, Reception, and Canon Formation.* He is currently at work on two books: *Recollections in Tranquillity: The Collected Author and the Institutionalization of Romanticism* and *A History of British Theatre: Staged Conflicts.* He is coeditor of *The Broadview Anthology of Romantic Drama* and Samuel Coleridge and William Wordsworth's *Lyrical Ballads 1798 and 1800.*